WRITING ARCHAEOLOGY

Second Edition

To Mitch Allen

With thanks for friendship and countless hours
talking about writing.

Stirred now by the Muse, the bard launched out
in a fine blaze of song . . .

—Homer, *The Odyssey*

I can assure you that I cannot get enough good serious nonfiction
books to meet publisher interest. . . . The solution is not to give up
writing but to understand the new realities and make reasonable
adjustments to them.

—Susan Rabiner, *Thinking Like Your Editor*

WRITING ARCHAEOLOGY

Telling Stories about the Past

Second Edition

Brian Fagan

12/19/2010

Left Coast
Press Inc.

Walnut Creek, California

Left Coast Press Inc.

LEFT COAST PRESS, INC.
1630 North Main Street, #400
Walnut Creek, CA 94596
http://www.LCoastPress.com

Library of Congress Cataloging-in-Publication Data

Fagan, Brian M.
  Writing archaeology : telling stories about the past / Brian Fagan.
    p. cm.
  Includes bibliographical references.
  ISBN-13: 978-1-59874-608-2 (hardcover : alk. paper)
  ISBN-10: 1-59874-608-1 (hardcover : alk. paper)
  ISBN-13: 978-1-59874-609-9 (pbk. : alk. paper)
1. Archaeology—Authorship. 2. Report writing. 3. Archaeological litera-
ture—Publishing. I. Title.
  CC82.6.F34 2010
  808.8'0358301—dc22

                                    2010036304

Printed in the United States of America

♾ The paper used in this publication meets the minimum requirements of American National Standard for Information Sciences—Permanence of Paper for Printed Library
Materials, ANSI/NISO Z39.48–1992.

CONTENTS

PREFACE

WRITING ARCHAEOLOGY is about just that-writing articles and especially books on archaeology, mostly for wider audiences rather than the narrow coterie of fellow specialists. This is not a book about subtle nuances of style or literary genres, but a brief look at the harsh practicalities of writing. It's an essay on self-discipline, on the habit of writing, and on the process of having an idea and turning it into an article or a book. The emphasis is on the process, not on creativity and all the often mythic mumbo-jumbo that clutters literary magazines and seminars at writers' conferences. This book is aimed at archaeologists who want a practical guide about how to write productively both in the academic world and in horizons beyond the specialist arena. There's much here that's of value to academic authors, too, as well as to students writing dissertations. Indeed, I've added a chapter on academic writing to this edition. Nevertheless, this book has no pretensions about being a guide to intensive specialist writing. For that, you should consult Howard Becker's *Writing for Social Scientists* (1986), Robin Derricourt's admirable *Author's Guide to Scholarly Publishing*, and other widely available titles.

Following the enthusiastic reception of the first edition, I've made few changes to the second one. However, in response to reader requests, I've added a chapter on academic writing, another on how to strategize publication from a dissertation, and a third on the exciting new field of digital publication, which promises to revolutionize both publishing and writing in fundamental ways.

The book begins with an introduction to general writing, followed by a chapter on articles, columns, and other shorter writing assignments. Then six chapters take you through the process of writing a general book, from the initial idea through writing the proposal, the first draft, revisions, the final manuscript, and production. These chapters are aimed at people wanting to write a general book for the trade market. Chapter 9 discusses another genre, the textbook, a publishing world unto its own. The most common question asked by younger scholars concerns publication possibilities from a dissertation. I offer some advice on this in Chapter 10. Finally, Chapters 11 and 12 discuss academic writing and writing for the digital world. A short resources section provides some guidance on basic sources for writers as far as style, markets, and other basics are concerned.

All of this has one objective—to get you writing. There is only one way to do it, only one mantra. Just write, write, write! If this book helps you get started and explains how to go about it, then its work is done.

Write! Write! Write!

ACKNOWLEDGMENTS

Mitch Allen has been an esteemed friend and colleague for many years. We've exchanged ideas and worked on many projects together in wonderful harmony. This book was originally written as a celebration of his new publishing house, Left Coast Press, Inc. and, in its second edition, is a tribute to the press's success. The chapters result from sustained discussion that distills our collective experience. The least I can do is dedicate it to him, with thanks for his encouragement.

My thanks to Kris Hirst and George Michaels, who read Chapter 11 and saved me from many grievous sins. They know far more about cyberspace than I do. Shelly Lowenkopf read the manuscript, talked me through it, and contributed numerous sound ideas, as he does to all my writing. He is a true friend, who was a fountain of inspiration for the manuscript. My thanks, too, to the many editors who have encouraged me and taught me how to write over the past forty-five years. They have been a wonderful part of my life.

Brian Fagan
Santa Barbara, California

COME, LET ME TELL YOU A TALE

Rule 1: Always tell a story.

In 7000 B.C., a small group of hunter-gatherers camped in a sandy clearing near Meer, in northern Belgium. One day, someone walked away from camp, sat down on a convenient boulder, and made some stone tools, using some carefully prepared flakes and lumps of flint he or she had brought along. A short time later, a second artisan sat down on the same boulder. He or she also had brought a prepared flint [rock], struck off some [flakes], and made some [drills]. Later, the two stone workers used their finished tools to bore and groove some bone. When they finished, they left the debris from their work lying around the boulder. . . . The second stone worker was left-handed. (Fagan 1995:23)

WHEN THE BELGIAN ARCHAEOLOGIST David Cahen excavated the Meer site 9,000 years later, all he found were some amorphous scatters of stone-tool debris, seemingly unpromising material for telling the tale of the two stone workers. But by plotting the position of every chip and flake, and by using retrofitting and use-wear analysis, Cahen reconstructed a convincing story of Stone Age daily life.

How did he know that one of the individuals was left-handed? Use-wear expert Lawrence Keeley examined the flint borers under low- and high-power magnification, and found abrasion marks from counterclockwise twisting on some of them—only a left-handed user could have employed an awl this way.

Cahen and his colleagues work far from the limelight and publish their work in specialist journals and monographs. Few archaeologists other than fellow specialists peruse their work, yet much of this kind of research unlocks the past by linking it to our own lives through things we have in common. Left-handedness is a good example. I've found that lecture audiences are electrified by the Meer story. When I talk about ancient left-handedness, they gasp. As I take them step by step through the research, you can hear a pin drop, especially when I show them a picture of left-handed abrasions. The power of this seemingly prosaic tale comes not from the events, but from the ingenious, logical way in which an archaeologist pieced it all together.

The story can be a trivial event, or it can involve a larger historical theme, like that of the camel. Strange that a camel saddle changed history, but it did. South Arabian nomads first domesticated camels sometime before 2500 B.C., but ten centuries passed before camels came into common use. The problem was not the camel, but the saddle. The first Arabian camel saddles were mounted over the animal's hindquarters. Seated near the rear of the beast, the rider lost the major strategic advantage of the camel—the height of its master above the ground. The first breakthrough came with the development of the North Arabian saddle sometime during the five centuries before Christ. This is a rigid arched seat mounted over the camel's hump that distributed the load evenly over the animal's back. Now a rider could sling packs from both sides of the saddle and, even more important, could fight from camelback.

For centuries, the powerless camel breeders and owners had been the servants of the producers and buyers of frankincense and other commodities. Now they found themselves in the proverbial saddle, armed masters of the long caravan routes that crisscrossed southwestern Asia and the Nile Valley. Profits from the caravan trade flowed into their hands; Petra in the Jordanian desert became the first of the great caravan cities. So efficient was the camel with the North Arabian saddle that wheeled carts effectively vanished from southwestern Asia for many centuries.

Again, a near-invisible artifact in the archaeological record makes for a compelling story and explains the seemingly mysterious disappearance of wheeled carts over a wide area for many centuries.

Writing archaeology for a general audience requires storytelling, not the just-so stories rightly castigated by legions of archaeologists, but compelling narratives based on the best scientific data available.

Storytelling

Come, let me tell you a tale: the phrase conjures up images of a storyteller by a campfire or a grandfather reading to his grandchildren in a deep armchair. Since the beginnings of speech, humans have passed beliefs, folklore, and essential skills from one generation to another by storytelling. The Old Testament is a series of stories and teachings. So are *The Epic of Gilgamesh* and Homer's great poems. The Greek authors Herodotus and Thucydides were expert storytellers. Great nineteenth- and twentieth-century historians like Francis Parkman and Samuel Eliot Morison were consummate masters of stirring narrative: "A brave wind is blowing and the caravels are rolling, plunging and throwing spray as they cut down the last invisible barrier between the Old World and the New . . ." (Morison 1942:226).

Who else but Morison could communicate the excitement of Christopher Columbus's landfall in the Indies in so few words? Only a handful of archaeologists have ever tried to write such powerful narrative. Howard Carter wrote wonderfully understated accounts of Tutankhamun's tomb, including these famous sentences:

> The very air you breathe, unchanged through the centuries, you share with those who laid the mummy to its rest. Time is annihilated by little intimate details such as these, and you feel an intruder. (Carter and Mace 1923:124)

There's an immediacy about Carter's writing that makes you feel you were in on the discovery.

Some of the best archaeological writers worked in the nineteenth century, notably Englishman Austen Henry Layard, who excavated at Nimrud and Nineveh in Iraq. He wrote of his excavations in 1849:

> The great tide of civilization has long ebbed, leaving these scattered wrecks on the solitary shore. . . . We wanderers were seeking what they had left behind, as children gather up the coloured shells on the deserted sands. (Layard 1849:112)

"What they had left behind": Layard's five words epitomize the challenge of the archaeologist as a storyteller. Not for us the rich chronicles of medieval Spain or the blow-by-blow accounts of the Battle of Trafalgar or the events of 1776. As the British archaeologist Stuart Piggott reminded us a half-century ago, archaeology is "the science of rubbish." Our archives, our blow-by-blow accounts, come from the trivial detritus of history. This debris comes in many forms: stone flakes and finished projectile points, potsherds, grinding stones, house foundations, beads, animal bones, and humble seeds. These artifacts and food remains are the equivalent to the historian's archives. Like the crabbed records of medieval monasteries or obscure government documents from a century ago, they are often unintelligible to anyone but the handful of experts who delve into them.

We've largely forgotten how to tell stories about the past. In an era of daunting specialization and high-tech science, we archaeologists, like other scholars, communicate in tongues alien to the outsider—laws of association, stratigraphic profiles, processual approaches, and so on, to say nothing of obscure cultural names like Acheulian, Bandkeramik, Clovis, and Mississippian. Then there are technical terms like "prepared core technique," "reductive technology," and "slip." It's as if we have a secret code for communicating with one another, which is unintelligible to the world at large. This is a product of the intensely specialized nature of twenty-first-century archaeology, where people working in one area will use a completely different set of cultural terms from researchers laboring only a few hundred miles away. There's also a need for precise terminology, so that everyone in a particular specialty knows exactly what the others are talking about. Add to this the generally appalling standards of writing in archaeology, and it's easy to understand the huge chasm between archaeological research at the technical level and our wider audience. And there is such an audience, just as there is for astronomy and Civil War history—readers passionate about the past, often well informed, and anxious to learn more. As another British archaeologist, Barry Cunliffe, remarked some years ago, archaeology as we practice it is like an unperformed play, waiting in the wings for the actors to appear on stage.

The challenge is to make the past come alive, using an archaeological record that is often, to put it mildly, unspectacular.

All archaeological sites, all finds, have a story to tell, not about artifacts and food remains, house foundations or fortifications, but about the people behind them. Much general writing in archaeology buries itself in dreary lists of artifacts and turgid journeys from one obscure archaeological site to the next. I, among many others, have been guilty of this.

We forget that all archaeology is the result of human behavior, of people like ourselves. Like us, they were born and grew up, loved, got married, had children, and died. They negotiated with one another, quarreled, sometimes got in fistfights, were occasionally hungry, and revered their ancestors. We have a common bond over the centuries and millennia, epitomized by the left-handed stone worker at Meer. Archaeologists have rich, compelling stories to tell, but all too often we shy away from the challenge.

Approaching a Story

Duncans Point, near Bodega Bay, 6000 B.C.: the hunters sidle ever closer, moving quietly on the slippery rocks, spears and heavy wooden clubs in hand. Well spread out, sure of foot, and carefully downwind, they move in so close that they can literally touch their prey. Then the killing begins. Quick spear thrusts, brutal blows with the wooden clubs as the men set about them left and right, trying to kill every seal in reach. Many of the adult males escape quickly, wriggling to safety in the breakers. The hunters take the mothers and their young, also older beasts, which wake up confused, to stare death in the face.

A few hectic moments and the hunt is over. The men club any
dying beasts, then carry and drag away the fresh carcasses. They skin
and butcher them on the low cliff above the rookery. Back at camp,
they hang strips of meat out to dry in the afternoon sun, while the
women peg out the seal skins and scrape them clean. (Fagan 2003:62)

This brief account of a seal hunt is reconstructed from the finds at a
coastal site in northern California. The scenario is fictional but based
firmly on the available archaeological evidence. Note the use of the
words "slippery," "downwind," and "literally" to make the environment
come to life and to dramatize the strategy of the hunt, which requires
the hunter to stalk his prey from downwind with great expertise. I
wrote this reconstruction as the hook for a chapter on early coastal
settlement in a book on ancient California commissioned for the general public. The raw material for the chapter was far from exciting, but
the brief reconstruction set the stage for the story that followed.

Telling any archaeological tale convincingly is hard, especially
when the raw material for the narrative is both sparse and visually dull.
If you want a quick analogy, make a list of six convenient objects close
to your computer—in my case, an electric clock, a pencil, a stereo
remote, a paper clip, and a box of blank CDs. Then try to construct a
meaningful story about the person who owned them. A seemingly
impossible task, until you remember Sherlock Holmes and his brilliant
capacity for logical observation. The image of the archaeologist as a
kind of detective piecing together clues from arcane finds is a well-
worn cliché, but it must be admitted that there is some truth in it.

You can approach your storytelling in many ways, but every story
needs a plot, a central thrust that carries the reader through to a satisfying end. I always remember a New York editor quoting *Alice in Won-
derland* at me, the immortal words of the King of Hearts: "Begin at the
beginning, go on to the end: then stop." How right both my editor and
the King were! An article, each book, every chapter needs a beginning
and an outcome—if nothing else, a link to the next chapter. This
means that you must have a genre that is appropriate for the story.
There is no set formula, no easy solution. With every book I have written, I have spent an enormous amount of time thinking about, and
sometimes agonizing over, the best potential approach to the story.

There's a bewildering array of options, but everything depends on the subject matter. Ivor Nöel Hume is a superb excavator, an exemplary historical archaeologist, and a wonderful writer. He is most famous for his excavations at Martin's Hundred, a small Colonial settlement near Williamsburg, Virginia, attacked by Indians on March 22, 1622. He spent five years excavating the village and perusing court and legislative records to fill in historical details. In a cellar filling, his excavators found a short length of twisted and glued golden wire called a "point," a type of decoration sported by the gentry and military officers of the early seventeenth century.

In *Martin's Hundred*, his popular book on the subject, Nöel Hume brings his carefully reasoned archaeological detective work on the gold thread to life. He makes the reader feel as if he or she is at his side as he finds the thread in the foundation, then identifies it as an ornamental "point" worn on gentlemen's clothing. He researches early seventeenth-century costume in England, then learns of a Virginia Council resolution of 1621 that permits only "ye Council & heads of hundreds to wear gold in their cloaths" (Nöel Hume 1982:60). William Harwood, the head administrator of Martin's Hundred, had signed the resolution. Could the thread have been his property? The case was a weak one until Nöel Hume's team unearthed a cannonball in the same house:

> Fortunately William Harwood's immortality does not hang solely by a thread. We found another, more substantial link in the form of a cannonball. . . . In the 1625 census, Harwood was the only person in Martin's Hundred listed as possessing a "peece of Ordnance, 1 wth all things thereto belonging," and nothing belonged more than a cannonball. On the other hand, does one ball make a cannon? Who can say that someone did not borrow the ball from Harwood's magazine and use it to grain wheat into flour? (Nöel Hume 1982:63)

In this piece of deceptively effortless writing, the reader becomes a detective at the author's side and shares in the triumph of identification, also in the legitimate questions about it. Trivial historical detail, perhaps, but a marvelous example of good archaeological writing and storytelling.

Martin's Hundred is an example of the personal approach to archaeological writing. Nöel Hume writes a first-person account that has an immediacy that works well. Take an archaeologist who feels strongly about his finds and can write, and you will find the most compelling stories of all.

An increasing number of science journalists have come to archaeology in recent years. They often meld discoveries with stories about the archaeologists in field and laboratory. The reader embarks on a journey of discovery through the eyes of the scientists engaged in the research. This kind of storytelling mingles a first-person approach with serious science, highlights personality traits, even dress, to make the subject matter come alive. This approach was fashionable in the days of the titanic disputes between different factions of paleoanthropologists back in the 1970s and 1980s. Large grants and powerful egos were at stake, the potential readership for science writers enormous. It's questionable whether the public airing of academic quarrels did the field any good. Fortunately, things have calmed down now.

Sometimes, a professional writer will team up with an archaeologist. James Adovasio, a noted first-Americans scholar, teamed with a freelance writer to craft a highly personal account of a subject that was heavy on feelings, interpersonal relationships, and quarrels, while at the same time making a case for early settlement of the New World (Adovasio and Page 2002). *The First Americans: In Pursuit of Archaeology's Greatest Mystery* is a lively account of an often arid subject with few spectacular finds, but the personalities and disputes sometimes crowd out the archaeological story.

Some accounts of major research projects and excavations involve teams of scholars working on a common problem. Science writer Michael Balter wrote a book about the early farming settlement at Çatalhöyük in Turkey, a spectacular site with houses and shrines. Instead of writing a straightforward account of the excavations, Balter chose to develop a story around the diverse personalities and intellectual biases of the major participants. They named him the "project biographer." *The Goddess and the Bull: Çatalhöyük: An Archaeological Journey to the Dawn of Civilization* weaves archaeobotany and other scientific approaches together with details about the archaeologists, creating a book that is unusual and perhaps tells you more about the scholars than about the site itself. Here's an example of Balter's approach, which leads from the personal into science:

Christine Hastorf was back after a year's absence. Christine had not come to Çatalhöyük for the 1995 season. Her teaching load at Berkeley, her ongoing archaeobotanical work in South America, and the responsibility of caring for Nicky and Kyle had been more than enough to keep her busy that year. Ian had replaced her temporarily with an archaeobotanist from the Institute of Archaeology in London, Ann Butler, who built the project's first flotation machine with the help of a local village blacksmith. The basic principle behind flotation is simple: charred plant remains . . . tend to float in water. (Balter 2004:145)

Despite Balter's fascinating book, the best archaeological writing comes from archaeologists themselves, for they bring their passion, and an immediacy, to the story that works superlatively well in expert hands. The English archaeologist Francis Pryor is a master at this genre—witness his *Britain B.C.: Life in England and Ireland Before the Romans*, a highly personalized account of British prehistory in which he draws freely on his unrivaled experience of waterlogged sites. Pryor is what I would call a "comfortable" writer, one who is not afraid to share his feelings and thoughts, his moments of inspiration, with the reader. He's also an expert sheep farmer, apart from being a bulldozer operator of legendary acumen. He draws freely on his experience as a sheep farmer to write about the past:

> The archaeology of fields and farming is something that has kept me busy for thirty years. I can't say precisely why the subject fires my imagination, but when we lamb our flock in March there are times, sitting late into the night by a ewe that's either a first-time mother or an old girl having problems, when I'm acutely aware that people four or five thousand years ago must have experienced closely similar anxieties and emotions. (Pryor 2003:302)

Vivid stuff, and the kind of archaeological writing that strikes a chord, even with readers who have little interest in the past. Again, like left-handedness, the sheep farmer's plight resonates across the millennia.

Drawing on firsthand experience is an excellent way to bring a story to life.

Constructing a Story from Nothing

But what happens when, as is usually the case, there is no personal involvement in the research, where you are writing a general synthesis or embarking on a topic that covers a long period of time or a huge area? Once you have completed your reading, interviews, and museum and site visits, you face the problem of constructing a story from an outsider's perspective. Expect to find yourself floundering for a while as you try to strike the right balance between overall theme and detail, vivid reconstruction, and responsible science. It is never easy—witness the case of the California milling stones.

Some years ago, I was commissioned by the Society for California Archaeology to write a popular archaeology of California from the earliest times up to the arrival of the Spaniards. The archaeological record for the state is confusing, unspectacular, and published in a diverse, often obscure literature, which defies any form of conventional narrative. I could have chosen to write an archaeological culture history, but this would not appeal to the general audience the society had in mind. Instead, I elected to tell selective stories covering the major developments of the past 11,000 years.

I soon discovered that 7,000 years of these eleven millennia were marked by little more than thousands of stone flakes and milling stones used to process seeds from *Salvia* and other wild plants. History wrought in milling stones is like encountering a black hole in space. At best, we have only a blurred impression of their makers. How, then, could I possibly write an interesting story about crudely shaped rocks with a flat surface smoothed by hours of grinding, found everywhere that hunter-gatherers paused to collect wild grasses?

Baffled by the challenge, I cast around. Fortunately, I have a dispassionate friend, a fellow writer, who listens to my stories, critiques them, and offers ideas and inspiration. He knows my foibles, my moods, and my moments of literary despair, like the one that descended on me as I contemplated 7,000 years of milling stones. We batted the idea around and around—visual impressions, the kinds of foods processed on the stones, sounds. Sounds. . . . A flash of inspiration came and I remembered a long forgotten meal in Central Africa's Zambezi Valley prepared on a milling stone. We ate mongongo nuts prepared by our host's wife. She cracked the nuts on the milling stone, then

> started milling the nuts on the same stone with a coarse grinder, just a convenient, rounded boulder from the nearby river. Scrape, scrape, scrape: The sound filled the clearing for a long time, as she added more and more nut fragments to the coarse meal under the grinder, then sweeping the increasingly fine meal into a convenient wooden tray. (Fagan 2003:91–92)

This long-forgotten meal turned out to be a wonderful jumping-off point for talking about the milling stone, an implement of infinite flexibility in ancient California life.

Fortunately for an archaeological writer, ancient life was never static, always changing, so one usually has a chronological gradient for a story. This was a problem with the milling stone chapter, where almost all known milling stone sites were occupied only once, or are little more than a scatter of stone tools. I needed a site, or sites, that would chronicle the gradual changes in the lives of milling stone societies, which had to respond to the challenges of an increasingly dry world where surface water and pluvial lakes had become a rarity.

Serious writing is usually a solitary activity. Often your only companions are monographs, articles, and an ever-growing academic literature. In the case of milling stones, I needed inspiration from people who were in the field, actively involved with the archaeology of such societies. This called for a different kind of consultation, with archaeological colleagues rather than fellow writers. Quite apart from the published literature, they would know about unpublished sites, cultural resource management (CRM) projects, and other data that lie outside the public forum of academic literature. I happened to lament to a colleague in nearby San Luis Obispo about the apparent lack of stratified milling stone sites. "Skyrocket," he said. I had never heard of the site, which was unpublished, but he assured me that it was what I was looking for.

I contacted the excavators, Roger La Jeunesse and John Pryor, who introduced me to the site, named after a local mine, which is in the central Sierra foothills east of Stockton. Nearly 4 meters (12.5 feet) of sporadic occupation cover thousands of years of local history, from about 7200 B.C. to the mid-nineteenth century A.D. The excavators had uncovered a 3.1-square-meter (33-square-foot) stone platform built around a natural finger into marshy ground. Here the people camped and used milling stones to grind seeds for 2,500 years, until drying conditions forced its abandonment. Four thousand years later, their remote descendants built another platform, this time at the confluence of two streams. They resumed their ancient lifeway in a changed world, melding new foods and carefully elaborated technologies into hunting-and-gathering strategies that had worked well. Here was an engrossing story backed up with rich archaeological data that posed all kinds of interesting questions. What was so special about this location? Why did people build a new stone platform thousands of years after the first? Were they aware of the earlier one through oral traditions? Skyrocket was perfect for my narrative.

The combination of sounds (personal experience) and the discovery of Skyrocket, with its fascinating archaeology, made for a convincing narrative that had the potential to hold the reader's attention as we skated over 7,000 years.

The Hard Slog

Sir Mortimer Wheeler was one of the great excavators of the twentieth century, a flamboyant archaeologist of charismatic personality in the British imperial tradition. He transformed the archaeology of Roman Britain, investigated the Indus cities of Harappa and Mohenjodaro, and dug Charsada, a remote frontier city in northern India. His most famous excavation was at Maiden Castle in southern England, an Iron Age hill fort attacked by the Roman general Vespasian's Second Legion in A.D. 43. In 1937, Wheeler exposed traces of the savage assault on the eastern entrance. He found hastily buried war casualties, thousands of sling stones, broken weapons, and traces of a violent conflagration. Years later, he wrote a vivid account of the attack based on his archaeological finds, which ranks as a classic of archaeological writing, even if many of his conclusions have been invalidated by later work.

Vespasian moved his main attack to the somewhat less formidable eastern end. What happened there is plain to read. First, a regiment of artillery . . . was ordered into action, and put down a barrage of iron-shod ballista-arrows over the eastern part of the site. Following this barrage, the infantry advanced up the slope, cutting its way from rampart to rampart, tower to tower. In the innermost bay of the entrance, close outside the actual gates, a number of huts had recently been built; these were now set alight, and under the rising clouds of smoke the gates were stormed. . . . But resistance had been obstinate and the fury of the attackers was aroused. . . . Men and women, young and old, were savagely cut down, before the legionaries were called to heel and the work of systematic destruction began. . . . That night, when the fires of the legion shone out (we may imagine) in orderly lines across the valley, the survivors crept forth from their broken stronghold, and, in the darkness, buried their dead as nearly as might be outside their tumbled gates, in that place where the ashes of their burned huts lay warm and thick on the ground. (Wheeler 1943:244)

Effortless writing, one might think, but prose crafted with sedulous care through many drafts. Wheeler told me once that these were the hardest paragraphs he ever wrote, for they had to be based on the archaeological evidence, on the science of the day. Such writing is hard to achieve, a matter of lengthy practice, and a thorough mastery of a craft that seems alien to many archaeologists. Quite simply, it's a long, hard slog.

How Do I Learn How to Write?

So far we've talked about storytelling in the hands of experienced writers and about some of the ways in which they make a narrative live. At this point, you must be asking: how do I learn to write? By doing it, of course, is the glib answer, and the correct one.

Unfortunately, writers, like archaeologists, like to surround what they do with a form of mystique. They often use a jargon of self-justification, which, in its worst excesses, seems to be an attempt to set them apart from mere mortals. "Creativity," "inspiration," and "frustrated solitude" readily trip off the tongues of lecturers at writers' conferences. Some, in excesses of writerly zeal, even call themselves "artists." Yes, writing is a craft, the skill not easily acquired; but the mystique of the solitary writer wrestling with creative urges is nonsense. The reality of successful writing is different: solitary, yes, but invariably hard, slogging work, involving constant revisions. It hinges on the ability to look at the larger picture, coupled with the skill to bring it alive while delivering publishable prose to strict deadlines. Both academic and general writing require most of the same elements: narrative flow, descriptive language, active tenses, avoidance of jargon, and, above all, clarity.

Most people can learn to write with practice. It's just like working out. Your muscles will be stiff at first, but they soon become limber. Writing also gets easier as time goes by, to the point that it can become an addiction, even a compulsion. Many beginning writers take creative writing courses in the hope that they will learn to write, but there is really only one way in which you'll learn: develop a strategy to get yourself writing regularly, refine it, then forget the excuses and simply write, write, write. Later on, I'll take you through the intricate process of developing and writing a book. There you'll learn that the secret is to make writing a habit, preferably a daily routine.

Writing requires much more self-discipline than many people realize. It's just like going to the gym five days a week. You have to make it part of your routine, your schedule, and your lifestyle. If you do that, the need for excuses not to write will fall away and you will have overcome the single greatest obstacle to becoming a good writer. Grammar and sentence structure can be learned, style evolved with constant practice, storytelling ability refined over many years, but none of this is possible without at least a degree of self-discipline to get you started and keep you at it.

As part of the learning process, read as widely and promiscuously as you can. Read not for content but for style. Read some Victorians like biologist Thomas Henry Huxley, whose *Man's Place in Nature* (1863) is a masterpiece of argumentative, technical writing. Enjoy John Lloyd Stephens's *Incidents of Travel in Chiapas and Yucatan* (1843) on the Maya, Austen Henry Layard's *Nineveh and Its Remains* (1849) on ancient Nineveh, and Leonard Woolley's *Ur of the Chaldees* (1929) on the Ur excavations. Loren Eiseley was a wonderfully eloquent writer on archaeological themes. His *Night Country* (1971) is a classic. All of these authors, and many more, are worth your time. You can even read Winston Churchill if you like resonant prose, but be aware that he writes like an orator. Look for lively sentences, moving description, evocative paragraphs. Enjoy the changing pace of the writing, the way in which these authors engage the reader. You'll soon find approaches you like and begin to develop your own voice. This isn't to say that you should copy your literary mentors, but if you deconstruct their style it will help you develop your talents as an author.

Most people can become workmanlike, even exceptional writers by discipline and practice. Yes, it's hard, and some authors have more of a gift for it than others, but it's doable. This book is about the process of writing, the challenges, frustrations, and deep satisfactions of writing a book not for your colleagues but for a general audience. In Chapter 2, we start off by talking about an apprenticeship of writing articles, columns, and other smaller assignments. From there, we'll follow the process of writing a book from idea to publication.

ARTICLES AND COLUMNS

Rule 2: Deadlines are sacred. Meet them.

I F YOU'RE SERIOUS about writing for general audiences, the best way to serve an apprenticeship, as it were, before writing a book is to write for newspapers or general-interest periodicals. There's an insatiable demand for popular articles on archaeology of every kind and not enough archaeologically literate people to meet it. If you develop the contacts, you'll be astounded at the variety of outlets interested in your work. A few years of writing for their audiences is a wonderful way to hone your style and learn the realities of popular writing. It's a tough apprenticeship, but you learn how to write.

The Outlets

The newspaper and magazine world is enormous, even without considering outlets on the Web. Archaeology is a specialized niche, but one with a remarkably broad appeal to editors who publish articles about adventure, remote peoples, tourism, and science. Over the years, I've contributed to a bewildering array of newspapers and magazines—local newspapers in Central Africa, news magazines, travel periodicals, sailing journals, literary reviews, even to *GQ* (what a tourist should wear when visiting Egypt). I've contributed to design magazines, to Web-based newsletters, even the op-ed pages of the *New York Times* and *The Wall Street Journal*.

Most archaeology articles appear in humbler outlets, rather than in the leviathans of the magazine world—*National Geographic, Natural History*, the *New Yorker*, or *Smithsonian*. These journals have their stables of staff writers or regulars and are hard to break into unless you are fortunate enough to make a sensational discovery, in which case they may be on your doorstep.

Archaeology Magazine is a major outlet for reaching general readers and enjoys a circulation of more than 215,000, plus newsstand sales. The editors welcome proposals from archaeologists with interesting discoveries or potentially compelling stories. You can guarantee that anything you publish in their pages will be widely read within the profession and outside it, for *Archaeology* is affiliated with the Archaeological Institute of America. *American Archaeology*, published by the Archaeological Conservancy in Albuquerque, New Mexico, is another periodical that reaches a wide, but much smaller, audience. Most of their articles are by invitation, however.

Start local, with short articles for small newspapers and community magazines. Although space is generally at a premium, they often welcome contributions, especially if they don't have to pay for them. Much better to start at this humble level and develop a modest track record before approaching large national magazines, who will be concerned about your inexperience.

Once you have successfully published in these modest outlets, try widening your horizons. A good place to start is the op-ed pages or the travel section of a regional daily or weekly newspaper. National chains, of course, own many of the local papers, which means that they tend to use established writers and political commentators. But occasionally you can get lucky, especially if you contribute a piece on a topical issue like climate change in the context of the past, and so on.

All these articles, wherever they appear, will be between 800 and 1,200 words long, a nice length to cut your teeth on, but one that requires disciplined writing.

Op-Ed Articles

"Op-ed" is short for "opposite the editorial page." These are opinion pieces written by outsiders, not reporters, in their own words, on a wide variety of topics. Many op-ed pieces are, of course, political, but they cover a broad spectrum of subjects, though very rarely archaeology or cultural heritage. More's the pity, for we archaeologists have a lot to say about the destruction of sites and other issues, which pass the public by. Op-ed articles can be extremely influential, for they have the potential to reach important decision-makers. Most op-ed pieces are between 500 and 750 words, which may not seem like much but allows you to make a serious case and substantive argument. There's always a demand for good op-ed articles, but the competition is fierce, with many special-interest groups clamoring for attention. You're also competing with regular columnists and editors on staff.

James Alan Fox and Jack Levin, who surveyed opinion-page editors around the country, have some important hints for potential op-ed writers in their book *How to Work with the Media* (1993), which are summarized in the "Tips" section below.

Op-ed pieces are an excellent way of presenting reasoned arguments about a wide variety of archaeological topics. Archaeology rarely appears on op-ed pages, but it should—indeed it offers an angle that adds diversity to stories that appear on news pages. Your article can add depth, insight, and analysis to serious events, such as, for example, the looting of the Iraq Museum in Baghdad. There is always a place for an article on archaeology, heritage, climate change, and ways in which our science has an impact on the twenty-first-century world. It's a shame that more archaeologists haven't written for op-ed pages. They're a wonderful way of getting our message across to a broad audience.

TIPS FOR OP-ED WRITERS

■ Call and make personal contact with the op-ed editor. Some editors refuse to take such calls; others are a fountain of ideas and will give you guidance as to what types of articles interest them.

- Read op-ed pages for weeks before you submit an article. You'll get a sense of what the editors are looking for.

- Be provocative, even outrageous. Your hook must be focused, bright, and controversial. Be different. Don't duplicate syndicated writers—they never write about archaeology anyhow.

- Be relevant. Many papers prefer local subjects. For instance, an op-ed piece on improving access to Chaco Canyon will play well in Albuquerque, but not in Columbus, Ohio.

- Be timely—have a connection with news events.

- Plan ahead. Keep an op-ed piece on your computer ready to go when you see a news story that is relevant.

- Simultaneously submit your article to several outlets in different markets. However, some major newspapers like the *New York Times* will not consider op-eds that have been submitted to multiple outlets.

- Recycle your material and use it in different sets of newspapers—anniversaries of major events are a good hook here.

Submitting to Major Magazines

Submitting an idea to a national magazine requires careful preparation and an original, compelling idea. No one can predict, of course, what ideas will appeal to editors, for the shifting sands of fashion and public interest are never still. Generally, archaeological stories in magazines tend to fall into the following categories:

Sensational Discoveries

An unexpected find like the Grotte de Chauvet or the Lords of Sipán is always popular fare. The most sensational discoveries almost always appear in *National Geographic*, with the finder being asked to write the story. Early hominin discoveries are also popular with major science magazines.

Interesting Discoveries and Theories

This category covers everything from industrial archaeology to wet sites and the latest theories surrounding the Ancestral Pueblo. Unless the subject matter has a broad popular constituency—mummies are an obvious draw, for example—the story will most likely appeal to specialty magazines like *Archaeology* or *American Archaeology*. *Natural History* and *Smithsonian* sometimes carry articles on major sites or unexpectedly interesting projects—much depends on the originality of the idea and whether you are the actual investigator. Most archaeology articles belong in this general category.

Advances in Archaeological Science

Archaeological detective work using high-tech science interests many editors, especially if the science has relevance to such contemporary issues as climate change. Again, this is a niche category, but one where editors will consider unusual ideas and stories about bold experiments. For example, I've seen stories (mainly written by science journalists) on such innovations as carbon isotope analysis and maize from Chaco Canyon, tree-ring dating of Stradivarius violins, and studies of growth rings in shellfish from the Pacific Northwest.

Profiles of Archaeologists

This category appeals mainly to newspapers, but occasionally there's a market for a profile of a well-known, controversial, or interesting archaeologist, the emphasis being as much on the personality as on the career. Louis, Mary, and Richard Leakey are popular subjects, as is Don Johanson. The *New Yorker* ran a long feature on the controversial archaeologist Frank Hibben some years ago, and the underwater archaeologist George Bass is a favorite topic.

Contemporary Issues

Articles on how archaeologists re-create ancient agriculture or irrigation systems, or on how past societies adapted to drought and climate change, even to El Niños, can sometimes engage editors, provided there is a clear relevance to an important issue in today's world. *Atlantic Monthly*, *Harpers*, and the *New Yorker* have carried notably intelligent articles that involve archaeology and contemporary society in recent years. They tend to commission such articles rather than acquiring them over the transom.

Heritage and Travel

Archaeologists receive little training in heritage or tourism, which is astonishing, given the mushrooming demand for cultural tourism of all kinds. Nor is archaeological travel a major feature of the established archaeological magazines, with the notable exception of *Current World Archaeology*, published in England, which has made a point of catering to the knowledgeable archaeological traveler.

Travel is the most promising category for the beginning writer, once you have developed the necessary connections to place interesting material. No archaeologist I know of has written regularly for major travel magazines, for cruise-ship periodicals, even airline magazines. More's the pity, for we have some fascinating tales to tell.

There are, of course, numerous other angles, limited only by your ingenuity. A good idea will always sell. The key factors are persistence, fresh ideas, and developing networks of editorial contacts. Think outside the box. It's no use, for example, proposing an article on Mesa Verde, which is familiar territory; however, a proposal for a story about educational programs for the public at Crow Canyon Archaeological Center is somewhat more unusual.

Before you contemplate proposing a story to any outlet, be sure to read several issues of the relevant periodical, check their web site to see if they accept unsolicited story ideas, and consult a reference work like *The Writer's Handbook* to establish what kinds of stories they publish. It's obviously pointless to send a story on radiocarbon dating to a car magazine, but people actually do it. Now, an article on suitable vehicles for archaeological fieldwork might find a home somewhere. . . .

Proposing a Story

If you are approaching anything except a local publication, you'll have to develop a written proposal. Write an e-mail or letter, addressed to the editor (or managing editor) by name, which shows you have researched the journal. In your epistle, which should be short, to the point, and businesslike, briefly discuss the following key points:

■ Your idea, giving the major themes and examples you will use, as well as the personalities, if any, involved. Be engaging and specific, but above all be passionate, stressing in particular what is new and unusual in your story for the magazine's readers. Two paragraphs is sufficient. If the editor wants more, he or she will let you know.

■ Why should this story be written now? Two or three sentences should suffice.

■ Why are you the best person to write this story? Briefly mention your qualifications, why you are interested in the story, and your writing experience. What special skills and experience do you bring to the project? One paragraph, maybe two, is enough.

Resist the temptation to send a long, detailed proposal, or a completed manuscript. If you have such an animal, mention it in your proposal letter, so the editor can ask for it.

Your proposal (which may or may not require a self-addressed, stamped envelope—the magazine's proposal guidelines will tell you) will generate a variety of responses. There may be silence, or the proposal may be returned in your stamped addressed envelope with a computer-generated rejection letter. If there is some interest, you may actually receive a rejection letter from the editor, or from one of his or her assistants, offering polite encouragement to try with another idea in the future. If they really like your idea and can't find a home for it, they may even suggest some other ideas to explore—part of an editor's constant search for new ideas and fresh trends. Best of all, you may receive an e-mail, letter, or phone call expressing strong interest in the idea, or even offering you a formal assignment.

POINTS TO COVER IN A PROPOSAL LETTER

■ Your idea and story line.

■ Why this story should be written now.

■ Why you are the best person to write the article.

Expect rejection. It's part of every writer's life and is nothing personal. Quite apart from the dozens of writers vying for editorial attention, an idea that interests you may not engage others. All you can do is move on and try again with another idea, or peddle your original one to other outlets. Remember: good ideas always find homes. Every rejection gains you experience and, above all, a network of contacts for future ideas.

If Your Idea Is Accepted

Typically, editors will call or e-mail if they want to offer you an assignment. They will outline their expectations and what they are looking for in the article. However excited you are about your idea being accepted, listen carefully to what the editor is saying to avoid any confusion when you submit the article. Ask that they send you an e-mail or letter outlining specific expectations.

Eventually, you'll be sent a contract that spells out the fee (if any), allowances for expenses (if paid), length, deadline, and so on, but here are some points you need to establish for the average feature article:

Length

How long is the article to be? This will be specified precisely—say 1,800 words—or more loosely as 1,500 to 2,000.

Illustrations

Establish who is taking the photographs and how many are required. *National Geographic* and other major magazines will often assign a photographer to a project, to the point that the picture captions are almost a parallel story. Often, however, it's up to you. If reproduction fees are to be paid to a photographer or agency, make sure that the magazine pays for them. Most magazines draw their own maps and diagrams in-house, but you should check this. You will probably be expected to produce roughs for the artist.

Method of Submission

In this day and age, submission is usually electronic, but check if this is so. Also, be sure your word-processing program is compatible with theirs. Most magazines and publishers currently use Microsoft Word. When submitting in this format, you should specify which version and platform you are using. For instance, Word for Vista cannot be read by earlier versions.

Deadline

When is the article due in-house? Be careful here. Most magazine editors' lives revolve around immutable deadlines with printers, and they often work up to the last minute. Make sure that you have enough time to do a first-rate job and to make changes if requested. Beware of the last-minute assignment unless you have time to make changes literally at an hour's notice. Fortunately, major articles usually receive much more time than short jobs like reviews of museum exhibits or movies.

Expenses

Most magazines do not pay expenses, but in general their stories are not ones that require vast expenditures on your part. You should check, however, for some will pay travel and other expenses, or for phone calls if the story demands them. The larger journals do pay expenses, in which case you'll be subject to their normal policies. Be sure to find out in what format you should submit expenses.

Rights

Most magazines request first publication rights, which means that after your article has appeared in their publication, you can try and place it elsewhere. Others demand world rights in perpetuity. Check the contract carefully for this.

Fees

Don't expect to get rich writing magazine articles. There is no such thing as a standard fee. Some magazines pay nothing, or a nominal $100. Others pay by the word—some nationals as high as $2 a word or even more, but such high-paying assignments are rare.

Fees are normally paid on acceptance or on publication, usually the latter. If the article is contracted, but then for some reason not published, some magazines pay a kill fee, which is normally a proportion of the final payment. The article may not be acceptable, their needs may have changed, or, as once happened to me, the photographer can bungle. Kill fees are usually specified in the contract. Even the most experienced writers have articles killed on occasion, for reasons that are no reflection on their abilities.

Writing the Article

Every article presents different challenges, for the subject matter can demand a wide variety of treatments. For instance, writing an interview with, say, Lewis Binford or Ian Hodder requires a question-and-answer format, where linearity is not an issue and a conversational style is essential. An article on Chaco Canyon would require some form of chronological gradient to keep the reader on track, as well as a narrative that combines reconstruction with actual data. The possibilities are endless, but here are some general comments that may be of use.

Outline

There are authors who eschew outlines for books (I am one of them), but with a short article, they're essential: they help you develop a structure for your story and find the correct balance of ideas, examples, and themes from the beginning. I always develop the outline in two stages:

- A short outline in which I develop the overall story in skeletal form before doing the research.

- A comprehensive outline that provides the raw material for the article and a completely fleshed-out story based on the research.

The comprehensive outline is the blueprint. In many cases, I specify the number of words per topic and subtopic to keep the length under control.

Research

It's easy to go overboard on research and to lose yourself in a mountain of irrelevant details. The secret is to organize it all into a series of questions that match your skeletal outline. As you go through them, put the answers on index cards or into a computer file. You can shuffle them until you achieve a logical order.

For instance, if writing about Chaco, at some point you would obviously need basic information on Pueblo Bonito: sequence of occupation, dates, dimensions, and so on. Establish these facts on an index card (or computer file), note your source, and the data is in hand—no more and no less than you need.

As the research progresses, you'll find that there are a few basic sources that you might combine with your personal experiences from a site visit, interviews with researchers, and so on. This material should also be distilled onto cards (or in a computer file), even if you have additional information to add to it in a file of relevant materials.

As you do the research, always bear in mind the central themes of the story and don't go off on tangents.

Some magazines, especially major ones like *National Geographic*, employ fact-checkers to go over your article after you submit it. In this case, you may be asked to submit an annotated copy of the manuscript that provides all your sources, including quotes acquired during interviews. This is no big deal if you have kept careful research notes and developed the annotated document alongside your drafts.

Once you have a set of index cards (or computer files, if you prefer) that seems adequate to compile your final outline, go ahead and write it. If there are gaps, they will become apparent along the way.

Getting Down to the Writing

Take your article through multiple drafts. Remember that words are not a precious commodity; let them flow. My first drafts are always at least 500, sometimes 1,000 words or more longer than the final version, but that's all good insurance against omitting something important. To get a draft on paper, stick to a routine. I usually shoot for 500 words a day or so, paying careful attention to my outline. Think about writing a story as if you were telling it aloud. Don't worry about style; just let the words flow.

Once you have a first draft, let it sit for several days before returning to it. Before you resume, print out a copy, brew a cup of coffee, and sit down to review the draft as a whole. Don't sweat the details—think about the story. Does it flow logically? Have you produced a logical, entertaining narrative with a beginning, middle, and outcome? Are there gaps in the story, ideas that need further exploration? Above all, is your research accurate and well documented?

Take your time, and then sit down and rewrite your draft completely. Put a stickie on your monitor: LENGTH! LENGTH! From now on, you need to work to the specified number of words, at first within a hundred or so, tightening everything until the final version is exactly to length. Now you face stylistic issues and the all-important first paragraph, the "hook" that entices the reader into your story.

Hooks are important in books, but have a crucial role in short pieces, where you have to seduce the reader into the story in short order. They are difficult to write under the best of circumstances, even for the most experienced writers. There are no easy answers. You have to rely on your instinct and rewrite again and again. A telling quote often works well, especially if it sets the tone for the story. "The Assyrians have had bad press . . ." is a nice hook, which led to a fine article on the treasure of Queen Yaba of Nimrud in *Current World Archaeology*. You want to know why they had bad press. Another lovely one comes from Larry Zimmerman's *Presenting the Past* (2003) in the Archaeologist's Toolkit series: "Once upon a time in archaeology, grizzled, field-hardened professors told their students that you aren't a real archaeologist until you die with at least one unfinished site report." Zimmerman then recites an "awful truth": "Many of us who got into archaeology did so because it was the fieldwork and its discoveries that excited us more than anything else" (Zimmerman 2003:1). The hook plays brilliantly on the guilt felt by colleagues who wrestle with their writing and know they have to do it. Here's a typical National Geographic hook from my book *The Adventure of Archaeology*: "We have here a completely new and unknown world. . . . An empire that alters forever our perception of ancient history. How many archaeologists have spoken words like these?" (Fagan 1985:9). Immediately, the reader plunges into a realm of exciting discovery. The hook, and a satisfying ending, are the most important elements of a magazine article.

WHEN WORKING THROUGH THE SECOND DRAFT

■ Concentrate on the narrative and your style.

■ Use short sentences and active tenses.

■ Avoid jargon and use a minimum of technical terms.

■ Keep away from clichés and excessive adjectives.

■ Keep your style simple and to the point, vivid yet pragmatic.

■ Never forget that you are telling a story.

Once you have a second draft, ask someone to read the article for you, preferably someone who is not an archaeologist. Once you have the outsider's feedback, you are ready for a careful edit for style, spelling, and so on. Check the guidelines given to you by the editor and make sure you are following them. The magazine will copyedit the article, but that's no excuse for a casual submission.

Length

Keep to the assigned word limit, unless you have specific permission to go over by a couple of hundred words or so. Some editors like to have a cushion for editing purposes in-house, but don't count on it. In these days of word processors, there's no excuse for not keeping within limits. A good writer can edit down to any length, if necessary word by word. If you are having trouble with that last hundred or so, look for phrases like "the majority of " ("most"), "new immigrants" ("immigrants"), and so on. Enough said!

Above All, Meet the Deadline

Magazines run on tight deadlines. Every periodical's schedule depends on a reserved slot at the printer, during which each issue is produced. If the editors miss the deadline, their readers miss the issue, which is, of course, economic suicide. Editors work under severe deadline pressure all the time, and you do no one any favors by being late with your draft.

Everyone misses a deadline for reasons beyond their control, like a family emergency, but otherwise there is no excuse for not completing an article on time. It's unprofessional, and that's a label no writer wants. To deliver good material on time is in strict self-interest. If you do a good job and produce on deadline, you can more or less guarantee that the editor will come calling again with an offer of a new assignment. Writers who deliver on time are much valued.

A good insurance policy against late delivery: ask your editor if you can send in an advanced draft a few weeks early, to get editorial feedback ahead of deadline. Almost invariably, the editor will be delighted, and in many cases they will accept your article at that time and rely on in-house editing to clean up any rough spots.

After Acceptance

Once your article is submitted, the editor may ask for changes, or a partial or even complete rewrite, which may have to be completed rapidly. A complete redrafting is rare, but often editors see things that you have missed or that they know will appeal to their readers which you might not be aware of. This is a fascinating, and usually short, part of the process.

Once your manuscript is accepted, an in-house copy editor will go through it and make changes that bring your stylistic usages in line with house rules. They may also edit parts of your article quite heavily, for they are aware of what works with their readers.

Generally speaking, you will not see proofs of a commercial magazine article—things move too fast. The copyedit will be your last interface with the article, and sometimes you won't even see that.

More than any other type of writing, magazine articles require a high level of teamwork and an ability on your part to work harmoniously with editors. Please do not stand on your ego and fight for your every word like a lioness protecting her young. The editors will certainly rewrite sentences and paragraphs in the interests of accuracy, but there's no point in getting a reputation for being difficult. Inevitably, you're going to be unhappy with how some of your articles appear in print, but the litany "the editors butchered my text" generally does not hold water with any competent magazine. They know their market and their readers. All the same, I've had some disconcerting experiences, especially with last-minute assignments. For instance, I wrote a commissioned article on archaeological fantasies for a well-known magazine on short notice and submitted it, only to discover that the editor had been looking for something quite different. The fault was mine, for I had not listened carefully enough to his verbal instructions. And he, for his part, had not set down his expectations in writing. Rather than prolong the agony, I withdrew in favor of another writer. The editor was gracious about it, but I was mortified. On another occasion, I labored for weeks on a story about an art exhibit in New York, only to have the magazine completely rewrite the article, shorten it below my specified word limit, and completely change the thrust of the review. Clearly, there were agendas at work here—the magazine was New York–based—but the first time I saw the final version was when it was in print.

Let's explore some other writing assignments you might encounter.

Columns

Archaeologists rarely write regular columns, but if you get a chance to write one, grab it. A column is a forum for controversy and discussion, for the airing of opinions, and sometimes for just plain sounding off. If you get readers' attention and the columns are quoted elsewhere, you're achieving something.

A column will require that you produce 1,000 words or so month after month, whether you feel like it or not. I wrote a regular column for *Archaeology Magazine* for some years, and the discipline of writing it was occasionally painful. Sometimes I ran out of ideas and had to struggle to find something—like camel saddles—to write about. This is a task that you should undertake only for a few years. Inevitably your creative juices will dry up after a while.

If you are asked to write a column, insist that you have complete control over the subject matter. Beware of micromanaging editors who want to "approve" your subjects ahead of time. Almost invariably, this means that you are making important, even controversial points with the readers, and some editors don't like it. Good for you. Without complete independence—within, of course, the usual limits of decency—a column is not a column at all.

Encyclopedia Articles

An epidemic of reference tomes has descended on the book world in recent years, and encyclopedias of archaeology are proliferating.

Such works are expensive to produce and have relatively limited marketplaces, mainly libraries. I get an invitation to contribute to such a volume about twice a year, invariably a request for an article on something about which I know precious little. A recent request asked for a 1,200-word entry on "Race Relations in Prehistory." Needless to say, I turned down the assignment. I don't understand the logic behind the constant stream of archaeology reference books, few of which cover anything new or have anything fresh to add. Eventually, however, you're almost certain to be asked to write an article for one. It's worth doing so at least once, if only for the experience and to broaden your knowledge, provided the subject matter interests you.

The entry can range from a few hundred words to 5,000 words or more. A particular site may require no more than 250 words, the settlement of the world by *Homo sapiens* several thousand. Encyclopedias rely on economy of words to cover huge subjects. Your entry will probably be part of a hierarchy of articles subsuming, say, the archaeology of the Andes, and should be confined to the site, or whatever other subject matter you are assigned. Keep to the word limit, keep it simple, and edit out every superfluous word. Sentences should be short, and there is no need for a hook. Cover the basics like date, dimensions, and people involved, and eliminate finer detail. You may be asked to give a couple of sources. Select those that take the reader into more depth and have good bibliographies. Most encyclopedia readers are students, who want accurate, succinct information with minimal effort. Provide it to them.

Compiling even a short entry is time-consuming and not particularly intellectually rewarding. The payment will be nominal at best, for which you cannot blame the publisher, who confronts enormous costs, of which the authors are only a minor part. If you're lucky, you'll receive a copy of the encyclopedia. Assignments for *Encyclopedia Britannica* and other such major works are well worth accepting for the experience, as the topics are often challenging and sometimes receive lengthy treatment. For some years, I've written an annual entry on recent archaeological discoveries in the Western Hemisphere for the Britannica Book of the Year, published by *Encyclopedia Britannica*. I always enjoy writing this, for the assignment keeps me on my intellectual toes.

Any short writing assignment operates under the same rules as those for a book (which we will discuss next): writing is a habit; accuracy and multiple drafts are fundamental; and deadlines are all-important. Short assignments can be enjoyable, and they have the advantage of being a wonderful sounding board for book ideas that otherwise might never occur to you. With luck, you'll generate some intriguing ideas from your articles that will help the search for book topics, the subject of Chapter 3.

GENESIS

Rule 3: Write only about topics that passionately interest you.

EVERYONE, EVEN THE ARCHAEOLOGIST, dreams of writing a best seller. If you're lucky enough (or unlucky enough) to have a book reviewed in the *New York Times Book Review*, colleagues assume that you're making millions. Visions of Jared Diamond's *Guns, Germs, and Steel: The Fates of Human Societies* (1997), which has made a lot of money from sales in the hundreds of thousands, seem to fill their mind's eye. Few nonfiction volumes ever reach the lofty commercial pinnacles of Diamond's works, and those that do almost always take off in the marketplace by sheer chance. I have never written a best seller, but at least I have the satisfaction of knowing that my books have reached many people who have an interest in archaeology. And that's the real purpose of writing for a general audience.

Consider the mathematics. About 275,300 books appeared in the United States alone in 2008. Many of them should never have been published. Poorly written, badly edited, and of marginal interest to anyone, they fuel a bizarre publisher's mantra that worships quantity of titles rather than quality. Today, books proliferate in niche markets, sometimes with audiences in the hundreds rather than thousands. They include an unending torrent of academic monographs and that curse of the modern publishing world, the edited volume. This is quite apart from self-published books or volumes published only on the Web. So your chances of attracting the rapturous attention of tens of thousands of readers are small. Much depends on marketing and timing, but in the final analysis, it all comes down to the idea.

Trade Books

General books are part of what is known as the trade market, that is, books sold in bookstores, by mail order, or over the Web. Textbooks are a completely different genre, which involves specialist marketing through college bookstores. Writing a text means joining a different world, and we talk about this in Chapter 9.

Generally speaking, trade books are works of broad general appeal, which are sold to the widest market possible. The trade market includes fiction and nonfiction, each with specialized genres. Nonfiction includes biography, cookbooks, history, self-help, science, and so on. Archaeology is a loosely defined genre that overlaps into history and science. The best-selling nonfiction trade books in archaeology and history are those that cross several market boundaries. A good example is Mark Kurlansky's *Cod: A Biography of the Fish That Changed the World* (1997), which appealed to both history buffs and foodies with a combination of history and recipes. Dava Sobel's *Longitude: The True Story of a Lone Genius Who Solved the Greatest Scientific Problem of His Time* (1995) was another remarkable best seller for the same reason: it appealed to a broad audience of serious readers in astronomy, history, and science.

The general trade market is hard for an archaeologist to crack unless you have a spectacular new discovery of international appeal, a truly broad and original topic of wide interest, or a human-interest story involving prominent scientists and contemporary issues. Donald Johanson and Maitland Edey's *Lucy: The Beginnings of Humankind* (1981), about *Australopithecus afarensis*, is a classic example.

Most archaeology trade books are aimed at a narrower segment of the marketplace, although it's nice, of course, if they sell more widely. Go to any Society for American Archaeology or Archaeological Institute of America meeting and you'll find dozens of these volumes on nearly any archaeological topic imaginable. There's a strong tradition of general archaeology writing, especially in Britain, where the London publishers Thames & Hudson have long blazed a trail. They started the well-known Ancient Peoples and Places series in the 1960s, which now numbers well over 100 volumes, although the pace of publication has slackened in recent years. Other publishers have followed in their footsteps with varying degrees of success, as the competition has intensified. In recent years, university presses have been under pressure to publish more commercially viable books. Houses like California, Cambridge, Florida, and Oxford have enjoyed notable success with high-end general books aimed at a much broader audience than their usual academic readership. Nearly all general writing in archaeology is, in fact, serious nonfiction aimed at informed, highly literate readers. In this category, I would include general surveys of ancient civilizations like the Egyptians and the Maya, books on how to decipher hieroglyphs, travel guides (a genre unto itself), biographies, and books about important sites (Çatalhöyük is a good example).

In recent years, the number of high-end general archaeology books has proliferated to the point that the market is saturated, especially in regional books, such as titles on ancient Egypt, the Maya, and the Southwest, to mention only a few. Even in a marketplace that favors volume over quality, it's becoming increasingly difficult to obtain a contract for an archaeology book of broad appeal. Yet another synthesis of the Inca, the Moundbuilders, or underwater archaeology simply won't be successful. Many publishers now look for general titles that have potential application in the classroom, even in small, upper-division courses, but there, too, the market is crowded.

How the Trade Market Works

The trade market is a colossal hydra of ever-changing dimensions. Long gone are the days when publishing was a gentlemanly occupation of tweed-suited editors who nurtured their authors through long careers. Bookstores were cozy, quiet places owned by knowledgeable book lovers, complete with comfortable chairs, a fireplace, and, frequently, resident cats. Whether we like it or not, trade publishing is

QUESTIONS IN BOOKSTORE BUYERS' MINDS

- Is the topic a "hot" one in the marketplace?

- Alternatively, is the book likely to appeal to a broad cross section of customers?

- Is there a substantial niche market for the book?

- Is there significant backlist potential?

- Does the author have a track record of sales both in the trade market and in the chain?

- What is the price of the book?

now a cutthroat, highly competitive business where large conglomerates (like Random House), huge chains (Barnes & Noble), distributors (Ingram), and Web outlets (Amazon.com) rule. You, the author, together with your book, are a commodity, to be judged based on your contribution to the bottom line of these rapidly growing media conglomerates. Of course, some small publishers and independent bookstores are still flourishing, but the trade market is mostly in the hands of of large-scale marketing organizations.

Even the most expert publishers guess wrong on the marketplace, which changes almost daily. When will the South Beach diet run its course? Which Hollywood star will be the flavor of next summer? How big will the scrapbook-making trend become? When we were talking about this book, Mitch Allen, my publisher, likened the trade market to a black box, and he is right. There is no one key to opening it, but the entire industry is now geared toward sales and marketing.

In evaluating your book, the publisher is thinking more about potential markets and sales figures, print runs, and ways of fostering sales in bookstores, among the chains, and on the Web, than about whether your major thesis is right or wrong. Yes, a good idea and a quality manuscript are important, but the real consideration in the commercial world of general publishing is profit. No book proposal gets accepted without a thorough vetting, not only by your editor, but by the sales manager as well, who will often determine the title, cover, length, and price of your work. When I was commissioned to write a book on Egyptian tomb robbing many years ago, the publisher changed my original title *And They Spoiled the Egyptians* to *The Rape of the Nile* (1975) for marketing reasons. And they were right—the book did well.

Archaeologists have an advantage in this dog-eat-dog world. There are a limited number of books that grab the entire marketplace—a *Da Vinci Code* or *Harry Potter* appear rarely. More common is publishing for specific niches within the broader culture. And archaeology is a proven niche. There is an enduring interest in the past: in Egyptian pyramids, Maya temples, Viking sailors, and Greek statues. Titles on these topics are recycled continually, even if they cover little new ground. Some years ago, I wrote *Egypt of the Pharaohs* for the National Geographic Society, with photographer Ken Garrett (Fagan and Garrett 2001). The society's members bought more than 20,000 copies from the initial mailing, and many more have gone out the door since, largely on the basis of the stunning photographs, for the text was but a summary of Egyptian civilization. Because of this enduring interest, publishers are more inclined to consider books by archaeologists than by, say, linguists, chemists, or sociologists. Marketing demographics are reasonably well defined—they look for National Geographic Society members, frequent international travelers, Discovery Channel watchers, History Book Club subscribers. The key for you, then, is to show the publisher that a substantial portion of this group of people will be interested in the ideas in your book, even if you're not writing about pyramids.

The publishing and selling of books run on a seasonal cycle. Your book is placed on a list (fall 2011, spring 2012). Even before you finish writing, your completed author questionnaire (see Chapter 8) will have been used to write catalog copy and provide information for the sales representative's manual. Your editor will have presented the book at the semiannual sales meeting. A cover will have been designed and a price established. As you read the copyedited manuscript and proofs, the sales reps are making a case for your book with independent bookstores and with the large chains. The latter are especially important, for the chain buyers decide on tens of thousands of titles a year. Their yea or nay can be the key to success or the kiss of death for your book. They are well aware of market trends and hot topics and have a vast array of statistics on their customer bases.

Once galley proofs are in-house, the publisher will disseminate them widely to book club buyers, to book review editors, and to magazines, with an eye for excerpting. They will also solicit blurbs from colleagues and prominent people (see Chapter 8). All of this is designed to create a buzz for the book before it even appears. Much of the initiative may have to come from you, as publicity departments are generally overworked and are required to focus on their few blockbuster titles.

Your book will receive a specific publication date, usually after books arrive in the publisher's warehouse. In a well-choreographed book launch, the promotion campaign swings into gear (Chapter 8) just as the books are placed on store shelves. Advance sales establish the basic sales record of the book. If the work does well and sells strongly, the publisher may increase the marketing and promotion. If it languishes, then promotion plans will be scaled down, bookstores will return it by the boxful, and it will quietly die.

After the season is over, three or six months later, the books are pulled from the shelf and sent back to the publisher to make room for the next season's titles. This is the publisher's nightmare—how many of those books, so hopefully printed and shipped in September, will be cluttering up the warehouse again, unsold, in May? These are the ones that appear on the bargain basement table the next year. Some books—and archaeology titles often fall into this category— are retained as backlist, books that sell slowly but consistently over time. But the media frenzy is over, as are most sales. If you want to keep marketing the book after its season, you usually have to do it yourself.

The reality of the trade market is simple: most books have a short shelf life in the store unless they produce reasonable sales, and ware-house space is expensive. In these days of print-on-demand and a sat-urated marketplace, an unprofitable book soon dies.

The trade market is a brutal place, but we archaeologists are lucky: there's always room for new ideas, even about familiar subjects.

Having the Idea

The ancient Egyptians and the Maya have been the hoary favorites of authors and publishers for years. One would think the market would be completely saturated, but still the books keep coming—and they sell steadily, reflecting a fascination with things Egyptian and Maya that transcends a mere archaeological audience. An explosion in cultural tourism has fueled demand even for long-ago-published titles. Your search for an original, compelling idea will need to mine less well-traveled archaeological highways.

You spend more time thinking about book ideas and writing proposals than you do writing the end product. Generating an appealing, original idea has never been easy, and it's even harder in an era when hundreds of new archaeological books appear each year. Sometimes unusual subjects do well—witness Eric Cline's lucid history of Jerusalem, *Jerusalem Besieged: From Ancient Canaan to Modern Israel* (2004), and his *The Battles of Armageddon: Megiddo and the Jezreel Valley from the Bronze Age to the Nuclear Age* (2000) about the savage conflicts fought at Megiddo. Unless you have one of those rare "aha" moments, be prepared to spend many frustrating hours casting around for your idea. There are no shortcuts. It takes time and you'll reject idea after idea, some of them after hours, even days, of work. Worst of all, you may discover that someone else is already writing a book on the subject.

Writing is somewhat akin to real estate, in the sense that there is a fundamental mantra that drives it. In real estate, it's "location, location, location," a principle so fundamental that real estate agents repeat it three times. The author's equivalent is "Passion, Passion, Passion," repeated thrice with a capital P. Never write a book, or a general article for that matter, unless you feel passionately about the subject. If you want to know what this means, read Linda Schele and David Freidel's *A Forest of Kings: The Untold Story of the Ancient Maya*, a flamboyant, closely argued book about the decipherment of Maya glyphs. David Freidel writes:

> I am changed by this book. I cannot look at a Maya ruin now and think of the people who built it and lived with it as abstractions, an aggregate social force shaping the material world and coping with

the process of living. Now I see Maya faces, recall Maya names, look for clues to their intentional acts, their decisions, and the events of their daily existence. (Schele and Freidel 1990:16)

Heady words, but Freidel means them. *A Forest of Kings* is often speculative, frequently controversial, but it lives! The raw passion of the authors shines through every page.

Passion makes for good archaeological writing. Let passion guide your every step and your search for an idea.

Let's make a distinction at this early stage between "idea" and "concept." Take the case of the left-handed stone worker we mentioned at the beginning of Chapter 1. Perhaps a well-delivered lecture on the subject excites your interest and raises questions in your mind. How old is left-handedness? Was it as prevalent in ancient societies as it is today? What would have been the effects on a hunter pursuing large or small game, on his strategy, technology, and weaponry? You're intrigued enough that you decide to write a book on ancient left-handedness.

A book on ancient left-handedness is the idea. But how are you going to execute it? What is your fundamental thesis, your concept for organizing and writing the book? How are you going to discuss the idea in specific rather than merely theoretical terms? Obviously, a book on left-handedness in the past is impracticable, because, with the best will in the world, it's impossible to obtain statistics on the incidence of left-handedness thousands of years ago. Here your idea has foundered on the shoals of practicality, on a conceptualization that cannot be carried through.

When thinking about ideas, you cannot divorce idea and concept from each other. They are closely interconnected.

How, then, do you have an idea? Some books suggest themselves. Schele and Freidel's *A Forest of Kings* originated in the hands of an editor at a New York publisher, William Morrow. The idea was timely, the Maya civilization appeals to many people from diverse audiences, and the authors had a deep passion for the subject matter, something that is apparent on every page. Here the concept, the link between theory and practice, came from major archaeological sites and from newly deciphered Maya texts.

Unless an editor has an idea (and many of those are impracticable, even if the editor's job is to sign up promising ones) or the work is commissioned by an individual or an organization, you are on your own. But I always start with some basic criteria, which are outlined in the box below.

If you follow these criteria, you eliminate almost all possible ideas immediately, but the ones that remain will deserve serious consideration.

CRITERIA FOR A BOOK IDEA

■ Is the idea an original one?

■ Will it appeal to a reasonably broad array of general readers?

■ Is the idea a broad one?

■ Does it cross several disciplines?

■ Will it appeal to overseas as well as domestic markets?

■ Is it a subject that has not been covered by others in recent years?

■ Do idea and concept mesh closely?

■ Above all, do I feel passionately enough about the idea to write a book on it?

Armed with these criteria, and a general idea of what kinds of topics interest me, I usually embark on the search for ideas by immersing myself in copious reading, the more promiscuous and wide-ranging the better. For instance, on one occasion I contemplated a history of seafaring from the earliest times. So I delved into the rich literature on the subject, soon discovering that I was navigating in complex academic waters and through a veritable flood of competing works already in print. I searched for gaps and found but one in the popular literature, a history of non-Western craft, especially lesser-known sailing vessels such as Arab dhows, Chinese junks, and Pacific outriggers. In the end, the idea shriveled on the vine because the publisher I was working with felt there was not a large enough potential market.

In another instance, I had a vague idea for writing a book on ancient religions and how archaeologists study the intangible. Again, I retired to the library and spent several days rummaging through books and journals. In both the seafaring case and this one, I had a vague idea of where to start in the literature, but in both instances the search led me into ever more obscure backwaters of academic publication. As I worked through the literature on mother goddesses, ancestor worship, megaliths, and Andean shamanism, I realized that no one had written a popular account of how archaeologists approach the ancient intangible. Eventually the idea crystallized into a proposal, a contract, and ultimately a book, *From Black Land to Fifth Sun: The Science of Sacred Sites*, that journeyed to the realm "where animals talked and walked as men, untamed, unchanged, real people still" (Fagan 1998:1).

Once you have explored the literature and fleshed out a general idea into something more specific, you must step back and look closely at your level of passion for the subject. What intrigued me about the religion idea was that I had a surprising amount of firsthand experience of the modern descendants of traditional religions, which had the potential to make the book come alive. Once I had linked personal experience to the often arid literature, I felt my interest quicken, as I mentally joined example to example, personal experience to personal experience:

Deep in the Central African savanna, the drums mourned the Ila chief all night. One kilometer away, at our excavation camp near the Kafue River, we slept uneasily. I tossed and turned to the incessant drumming, musing on an elder who had died full of years, with hundreds of head of cattle to his name. Only two weeks before, we had drunk beer and talked, as men do, of women and cattle, hunting, spears and rifles. . . . We had talked of rain and the high grasses perfect for grazing, of the right to burn off a field to fertilize the soil. . . .

As the sun rose in a hazy sky illuminating a grey dawn, heavy with the smell of wood smoke from burning fields, the drums fell silent. The chief's five sons had . . . danced on the grave, and, as the fine dust rose, sent his spirit to the bush, thus returning their father to that land that had nurtured him and generations of Ila farmers and cattle herders before him. In a few months the chief would become an honored ancestor, one of those who had gone before—a guardian of the land. (Fagan 1998:1–2)

The Ila chief's funeral, still vivid in my mind, introduced the reader to a central theme of the book—the close relationship between the living and their revered ancestors.

Ideas flourish or stumble not on how you feel about them, but on what other people think of them. The bolder and more way-out the idea, the more important it is to share it with others before you set fingers to keyboard. Whom to talk to? Fellow archaeologists are obvious candidates, for they probably have some background in what you are discussing, even if they don't have specific expertise. Some of the best sounding boards are people with specialist knowledge. They have the ability to nitpick your idea and to drive holes in your concepts using sources or arguments that may have escaped you. A colleague whose expertise is, say, classical archaeology can be invaluable, too, because he or she will approach your idea with an open mind and usually no theoretical biases. Anyone outside your particular expertise is an admirable choice, especially someone who reads widely outside his or her own specialty. But do talk to people who are not afraid to disagree with you. The last thing you need is a yes-person. You need someone who will say "yes, but. . . ."

If you teach, an undergraduate or graduate seminar is an excellent forum for ideas. Upper-division undergraduates are sometimes a better critical audience than graduate students, who are often afraid to argue and disagree in classroom settings where the teacher can be seen as an authority figure. Many years ago, I taught an upper-division seminar on the contacts between Western and non-Western societies around the world during the European Age of Discovery. The participants explored various societies ranging from the Tasmanians and Tahitians to the Fuegians and Aztecs so successfully that they urged me to write a book using their case studies. This was nearly thirty years ago. *Clash of Cultures* (1977) started as a trade book, and then became a text, which is still in print.

What about the potential general audience? You can learn a lot from talking to friends, fellow churchgoers, even yacht club members. Lectures to small groups can be magical, a forum where you can expose your new idea to a wider constituency. I did this in an early stage of developing the concepts behind a book called *Fish on Friday: Feasting, Fasting, and the Discovery of the New World* (2006a) and received a truly electric response from the audience, who said that they had "never thought of this," "this" being the Catholic doctrine of eating fish on Fridays and its effects on history.

Lastly, there are fellow writers. These folks are an invaluable resource, because they have either experienced, or are experiencing, the same process of refining ideas. You may know writers already: ask them to coffee. If you don't, consider joining a literary group, such as a writer's lunch, but be prepared to sift those who just talk from those who write seriously. You want the serious writers. I'm lucky in that over the years I've drunk gallons of coffee with writers engaged in all kinds of literary activity, ranging from serious nonfiction to pop psychology and mass-market thrillers. The group is a wonderful sounding board for ideas, contacts, and critical feedback. On one momentous occasion, an idea came to me as we were talking. It was raining and we were talking about El Niños. "Why not write a history of El Niños?" one of the participants asked me. "There's nothing out there." The proverbial lightbulb went on in my head and a proposal led to a book—*Floods, Famines, and Emperors: El Niño and the Fate of Civilizations* (1999).

At some point, and many discarded ideas later, you'll have exhausted the potential of library research and discussion. Now it's time to get something on the computer.

The Passionate Narrative

Passion, passion, passion: you are passionate about an idea. Now you must set it down in a passionate narrative. Once you have a firm grip on the parameters of your idea and its conceptual framework, block off a significant amount of time, gather your notes, and write a preliminary narrative of the book you have in mind. As you gaze at the blank computer screen, bring two words to the front of your mind: passionate narrative. Then start writing.

The preliminary narrative is a personal document that you will share with only a few people—perhaps a fellow writer, maybe an agent. In it, you set down the story that is your book, gathering the various themes that form your concept, developing them, and honing them into a seamless tale. Here you really are telling a story, with a beginning, a middle, and a final outcome. Thrust distractions from your mind and imagine you are telling your story to a friend, sitting in front of a blazing fire on a winter's night, a glass of your favorite beverage close at hand. Remember that this is an informal document, whose primary objective is to set down your narrative in a form that is easily intelligible to an outsider (essential practice for the formal proposal that will follow) and that flows from one paragraph to the next in an effortless story.

I strongly recommend writing quickly and setting down a narrative that is a flow of consciousness. In this way, you'll give your passion full rein and come up with an inspiring narrative. Just make sure that you follow a logical blueprint, perhaps a brief set of topic headings and paragraphs on a single sheet of paper that ensures you follow the plan in your head. Concentrate on getting the story set down, however messy it is.

Psychologically, the faster you get the story on the computer, the better off you are, even if you think you are writing garbage.

The story itself will unfold quite naturally if you have done your research and know what you are talking about. This is where the passion comes in. Relax mentally and tell the story, and pretty soon you'll find that your passion for the idea will carry you along, sometimes exuberantly. When developing *Fish on Friday*, I was astounded at how easily my narrative came together. I simply began with Christopher Columbus and Christ and the rest followed. Here's an extract from the beginning of the document:

> On October 14, 1492, Christopher Columbus, Admiral of the Ocean Sea, landed on the tiny island of San Salvador in the Bahamas. There he found naked people, "very well made, of very handsome bodies and very good faces." He was convinced that he had reached the outlying islands of east Asia, so he called the inhabitants of the new lands "Indians." At the time, "India" referred to all of Asia that lay east of India's Indus River, the little known lands that supplied all of Europe's exotic spices. In an era before refrigeration and adequate sanitation, spices masked the taste of rotten food and unwashed bodies, were thought to ward off infection, and treated

the sick. Columbus had sailed westward in search of gold and a new route to the world of spices. Instead, he landed in the Americas, a "New World more densely populated and abounding in animals than Europe, or Asia, or Africa."

Generations of historians have proclaimed Columbus the great discoverer, the first European to set foot in the Americas, propelled there by the seemingly open-ended rewards of the spice trade. They are probably wrong. Fifteen hundred years earlier, a forty-day fast set off a chain of seemingly unconnected events that led to the discovery of North America by fisherfolk long before Columbus made landfall on the Bahamas. This is a story of abstinence and fasting, of fishing consumption and holy days, cod, herring, and salt, above all of an explosion in fish consumption that ultimately brought the Pilgrim Fathers to New England.

"Then was Jesus led up of the spirit into the wilderness . . . and when he had fasted for forty days and forty nights, he was afterward an hungered." The Gospel according to St. Matthew commemorates Christ's forty-day, epochal fast of purification that led him to triumph over temptation. Abstinence and fasting have been one of the foundations of the Christian faith ever since. (Fagan, unpublished MS.)

The story just flowed out of me. To my astonishment, my first draft exceeded seventy pages. I now knew I had an exciting idea, but there was still a great deal to do. The narrative was loose, at times repetitive, loaded with passive tenses, and full of irrelevancies. But at least I had the passionate narrative I was seeking.

Once you have set down your story, let it lie fallow for a couple of days, then revise it and revise it again until you are satisfied that it is internally consistent and scientifically reliable and that the style is the best you can achieve. Look for unwanted tangents, repetitive arguments and sentences, and, just as important, gaps in your arguments and narrative. Yes, this is a working document for your benefit, but the more polished it becomes, the better use it will be to you as you write your proposal, which is the next stage in the process.

Let me stress that you are writing a narrative here, not a book outline. One way of thinking of it is as a letter written to a friend, a device

I've used successfully on a couple of occasions. At this early stage you should concentrate on developing your passionate narrative without the restraints of individual chapters and their content. When the time comes, your story should translate easily into both a proposal narrative and a provisional outline. But without having spent time on the initial run-through, the first telling of your tale, you'll find writing a proposal troublesome. And you have enough concerns with the proposal without worrying about the viability of your idea.

Once your narrative is polished and has been read by a couple of people, perhaps a colleague and an outsider, and if you still feel passionate about your idea, it's time to write a formal proposal for a publisher, the subject of the next chapter.

THAT ALL-IMPORTANT BOOK PROPOSAL

Rule 4: Treat the proposal as seriously as the book because you're selling yourself and your idea.

O VER THE YEARS I've read hundreds of book proposals for fellow authors and publishers. Only a tiny fraction of them are memorable, and those stand out for their passion, their original thinking, and their storytelling qualities. You know immediately that the chances of a really good book at the other end are high.

Invariably, these exceptional proposals result from hours of painstaking work and repeated drafts and from an utterly realistic appraisal of the potential popular appeal of their idea. This dispassionate analysis lies at the core of a successful proposal. Time and time again, I've had people sidle up to me at a conference and ask for my advice on how to get their book published—a popular book on Stone Age blade technology, an obscure site in Ohio, or some issue of interest only to a narrow constituency of fellow specialists. "The public will be interested in this," they proclaim enthusiastically. Wrong! They have made the mistake of confusing their own interests with those of the wider audience. Here's a good example from a wider writing universe: some years ago I had dinner with a charming couple who had just completed an eighteen-month voyage in a small cruising yacht around the South Pacific. They had visited dozens of small islands and had wonderful memories—like the hundreds of other people who have made similar cruises. "We want to write a book about our adventures," they told me. They were disappointed to learn that cruising stories like this are commonplace in the sailing literature and that the marketplace is saturated. I suggested that they write an account for the family archives, which they have now done.

A Book Proposal Must Not Be

■ An idea for a book that is too specialized and of narrow interest.

■ A hastily compiled, long, rambling document with no focus.

■ So short that the reader cannot judge the idea.

■ An attack on potential competitors, colleagues, or other theories.

■ Written in a style that is arrogant or talks down to the reader.

■ An assumption that it's a privilege to publish your work.

Remember: your proposal is as important as the book itself and is the key to success or failure in getting your idea published. Remember, also, that you are dealing with editors who work in the commercial world. Their books are expected to make a profit or at least break even. A proposal is, in many respects, a commercial document.

Writing proposals is one of the hardest tasks for an author. Some people excel at it, but I find it difficult because I'm too close to the idea and the material and it's hard to look at everything dispassionately. Be prepared to spend a long time on your proposal, whether it is destined for a university press or for a trade publisher.

Realize at once that you are working in an intensely competitive environment, far more so than an application for a federal grant, for example. The acceptance rate of proposals that are awarded contracts at some major New York publishing houses is somewhere around 1 percent. University presses are becoming more selective than ever. Faced with such odds, your proposal must stand out among the crowd.

Yes, the marketplace is highly competitive, but there's no need to be intimidated or to despair. The good news is that truly good, original ideas will always find their niche in the marketplace. But to sell them you must strike the right chord with an editor and the editorial board that stands behind him or her. With a good proposal, you can sometimes convince an editor to take a risk and publish something really bold—although this is becoming harder in today's bean-counting marketplace.

How Publishers Make Decisions

If you are submitting a proposal to a small publishing house, the owner may be your editor. Sometimes they'll offer a contract on the basis of a prolonged conversation and a short, proposal-like document developing the idea slightly more thoroughly. This is the way this book was developed, which saves a lot of time. But such a path requires considerable trust on both sides and a clear understanding by both parties of what kind of book is to be written.

In larger houses and university presses, the decision-making process is more elaborate. Your editor will present the proposal and a financial workup of the book, projecting sales, potential markets, possible print runs, planned retail price, and so on to the editorial board, which consists of fellow editors, marketing people, and financial executives. In the case of an academic press, the editor will also present peer reviews obtained from other academics. The board will make a decision after hearing your editor's presentation. No editor worth his or her salt takes a proposal to an editorial board without a high degree of confidence that it will be approved, but it is by no means automatic.

The questions that will be asked by members of the board revolve around several issues, which are outlined on the next page. A comprehensive, well-written proposal should answer many of these questions. A good proposal sells you and your book to the publisher.

SOME QUESTIONS LIKELY TO BE POSED BY EDITORIAL BOARDS

- Is the book about an exciting, topical subject? Does it say something new?

- What audiences will it appeal to? Does it have potential in both trade and classroom markets?

- Does the author have the qualifications to write the book and a track record of popular writing?

- Will the book have "legs" and become a significant backlist work with continued sales?

- Does the book have high sales potential? What will it cost for the house to acquire it in terms of author advance?

The Elements of a Proposal

Any book proposal requires a distinctive mind-set: you need to think not only about your idea, but also about why readers will want to read what you have to say.

A typical trade proposal, if there is such a beast, is between ten and twenty double-spaced pages long and has the elements outlined in the following box.

No standard blueprint for a proposal fits all archaeology books, nor should it. Much depends on advance preparation, on the thoroughness with which you have explored both your idea and its execution. This is where all your research and your passionate narrative come in, for, ideally, you can focus on crafting the proposal with the confidence that your narrative is thoroughly researched and ready for the wider audience. In these days of much shorter deadlines for books, much of your research will be completed before you start writing even the passionate narrative.

CONTENTS OF A PROPOSAL

- A narrative describing the idea and the themes of the book.

- Information about the author and his or her qualifications to write the proposed work—one page maximum.

- A discussion of potential core markets for the book. Obviously the publisher knows more about this than you do, but you should point the way—one page maximum.

- Details of any competing volumes in the marketplace—one page maximum.

- A provisional outline for the book, which briefly summarizes the contents of each chapter—three to four pages, sometimes less, sometimes more.

FUNDAMENTAL QUESTIONS TO ANSWER IN A PROPOSAL

n What about the book is new and exciting?

- What are the central themes and arguments?

- Why are you the ideal person to write this book?

- Why should such a work be published now?

- Who will make up the core audience for the book?

- Why will this audience find this book so appealing that they will buy it?

Let's examine the proposal package in more detail.

The Narrative

Assume from the beginning that the editor who receives the proposal will have questions, many of them revolving around the potential market for the book. You can sharpen the focus of these questions and even avoid some of them if you make sure that your proposal answers a series of fundamental questions, which essentially duplicate the concerns of an editorial board.

Treat these questions as a general guide for your thinking but refrain from answering them one by one with brief responses. This does not work. Your proposal must be a story. Think of it as a short, once again passionate, narrative that leaves the reader hungry for more.

Your proposal will be evaluated differently than you might expect. Academics are used to grading papers and being reviewed by, and reviewing, their peers. An editor will assess your proposed book but will also read between the lines. Do you command the material and the literature, draw inferences from the material, and develop fresh ideas? Do you pull the reader into the subject and make it come alive, without using unnecessary detail? Do you have a sense of narrative and good writing skills? Is there a passion behind the writing, a need to share this excitement with others?

What's the Book About?

Begin your proposal by describing what the book is about—the first of the five questions. Aim to inform and fascinate the reader. What's new in your idea? How did the subject come alive for you and why is it important? Include sufficient background to give the proposal a context for an editor who is probably unfamiliar with your subject matter. Editors need to know you can position your story on a larger stage. Bring the new ideas up to the front, so that the reader knows early on where your narrative is leading. Above all, what do you have to contribute to the subject?

Here, for example, is the beginning of the proposal I wrote for *Fish on Friday*. Notice that this draws on the passionate narrative quoted in Chapter 3:

> My previous two books discussed how sudden climatic shifts changed the course of history. *Fish on Friday* is the story of how one

dramatic change in what people ate, brought about by religious piety, set in motion a series of events that led inexorably to the discovery of the New World.

For most of us, the story of the discovery of the Americas has been reduced to its proximate event: the voyage of Christopher Columbus in 1492 in search of a shorter route to the spices of China and India. The only unanswered question seems to be whether credit for having discovered America should go to Columbus's crew or to Norse voyagers who earlier hopscotched the northern rim of the Atlantic—across the Norwegian Sea to Iceland, across the Iceland Strait to Greenland, along the coast of Greenland, then across the Davis Strait to what is now Canada.

Of course, the indigenous people of the continent would say no "discovery" of their continent was necessary—they knew of it all along—and that the first humans to set foot on it were neither Columbus nor the Norse, but their Siberian ancestors who crossed the Bering land bridge some 15,000 years ago. But whether Columbus's voyage was first, second, or just one of many passages carrying Europeans to the Americas, we can all concede that his expedition changed both European and American history in ways the others had not.

So, instead, *Fish on Friday* asks a different question: What had happened over the previous centuries that gave Columbus—and then Cabot, Hudson, and all the other maritime explorers—the confidence to venture straight out across the widest part of the North Atlantic Ocean? Remember, early European sailors hugged the coastlines, not only because they feared they might be carried over the edge if they sailed too close to the outer reaches of a flat earth, but because they knew their ships and sailing skills were no match for the unpredictable savagery of the open sea. What changed all that? And under what impetus? The answers, as this book will show, lie in a fish story. Not in the sense of the big one that got away, but instead the story of how an ever-increasing demand for fish changed western history. (Fagan, unpublished MS.)

At this early stage, I've identified the central topic of the book, also the notion that fish eating and fishing changed history by challenging the primacy of Columbus's and Cabot's discovery. The reader knows what the book is about.

Themes and Arguments

Once you have presented your idea, you must now discuss the central arguments of the book. This is not about the topic, which you have described, but about what you bring to the subject. What are you contributing to the debate on, say, the first Americans? What is lacking in existing interpretations? Here you must be specific: "This book will argue that the first settlers to move south of the ice sheets moved onto the Pacific coast with its exposed continental shelf, then foraged their way southward." You state your thesis, but you don't have to defend the hypothesis in the proposal—there's no space. But you've stated what your contribution to the debate will be, strengthening it by bringing in a couple of examples, for instance: "By examining newly acquired environmental information from the coastal shelf, the book will show that the first settlers could have subsisted off caribou, sea mammals, and fish in what was a reasonably bountiful coastal environment." Seduce the editor with your provocative arguments so he or she wants to sell your book. Stress why your idea and the thesis behind it are of interest to the general reader. You have to make a good case. I can think of dozens of archaeological topics that interest me personally, but are simply too arcane for the general reader. How many laypeople are interested in flotation or microliths?

Unless your editor wants to mine familiar territory, and a surprising number of them outside the mass-market world do, you will find it's the kiss of death to regurgitate familiar facts, interesting though they may be, to produce yet another dreary synthesis without any overall point. Archaeological bookshelves overflow with such forgettable volumes, some of them under my authorship.

Qualifications

Obviously, you need professional qualifications in archaeology—that's a given. But why are you the right person to write about your idea? A lifetime of fieldwork experience in Maya archaeology is fine, but why are you uniquely qualified to write about this particular subject? What gives you an edge? Specific research experience? Years of pursuing the answer to the question you pose? A track record of academic publication that makes you want to write a more general work? A record in public communication at a local or wider level can compensate for inexperience at trade writing. You certainly don't have to be a world authority on your topic. The archaeological world is now so specialized that you are bound to move into subjects away from your expertise. But you should be explicit as to why you are the right author. Here's an example, relevant to *Fish on Friday*:

> I spent my early career in Central Africa, working for many months among subsistence farmers as I carried out archaeological research. This gave me life-changing perspectives into the harsh realities of subsistence farming. At the same time, I became involved in the birth of multidisciplinary African history, which gave me an appreciation of the importance of the large issues of the human past. For the past thirty-six years, I have spent my career studying and writing about archaeology and various historical topics for general audiences. In addition, I have spent much of the past thirty years teaching undergraduate and graduate courses on subsistence economics, culture change, and ancient seafaring. . . . My years of field experience, and expertise with multidisciplinary sources of all kinds, make me uniquely qualified to undertake *Fish on Friday*, a book that requires a broad historical perspective, and multidisciplinary sources. In addition, I am a lifelong small boat sailor with offshore experience, something unusual in any archaeologist or historian. (Fagan, unpublished MS.)

This passage spells out my background, and also my sailing experience in some of the waters where the story unfolds—a useful bonus.

Audience and Competition

It's easy to go overboard, to wax lyrical over the enormous audience that awaits your book. Be realistic, for the publisher's marketing people know more about audiences than you do. The name of the game here is niches. Identify the core audience for your topic, one that is well defined, easily reached, and has devoted readers. Archaeology is such a market. Topics like Egyptology, Maya archaeology, mummies, and science and archaeology are all niches within this larger universe. If you know ways of identifying and reaching your niche market, be sure to address them.

Just how unique will your book be in the marketplace? You must be specific about competing books. Check listings on Amazon.com, Barnes and Noble.com, and other web sites. If there are several other books, emphasize the ways in which your book will be different. For instance, if you are writing about Çatalhöyuk and early agriculture in Turkey and southwest Asia, your book would have to be a different take from existing titles by Michael Balter or Ian Hodder. Be sure to look at all the potential competitors. Nothing is worse than an editor coming back to you asking about a competing book you have overlooked.

Personal Data

Some publishers want a complete curriculum vitae, others a brief summary. I would write nothing more than a half page or so, unless making a first-time submission to a university press, who, in any case, usually seem to want a full academic CV. Editors will always ask for more information if they want it.

The Provisional Outline (or Table of Contents)

The narrative discusses your idea, the themes of the book, your qualifications, and the competition. The provisional outline offers the publisher a fleshed-out table of contents. This is a critical element of the proposal, so plan to spend a great deal of time on it. You're not wasting your time, for the signpost of the outline will help you later when you research and write your book. Think of it as a chapter sequence that you have refined until it works.

Plan to go through numerous drafts of your outline, using your passionate narrative as a starting point. I always write a long outline first as a flow of consciousness. Some have been as long as twenty to thirty pages. Then cull, highlight, and edit it down into the final, shorter version. Ask yourself the questions in the following box.

Once you have completed a severe edit of the long version, you have the blueprint for the shorter outline.

Typically, outlines run to two or three single-spaced pages, with, at most, two or three paragraphs per chapter. Below, I discuss some important considerations.

QUESTIONS TO ASK ABOUT THE OUTLINE

- What are the key themes, the most telling details and anecdotes?

- Have you short-changed one theory at the expense of another?

- Is there material that you have omitted that ought to go into the narrative, perhaps as short bulleted highlights?

Show How the Book Is Organized

Remember that the purpose of the outline is to show how the book will be organized. In writing the chapter summaries, mention up-front the point each chapter is trying to make or the question it will discuss, then briefly summarize the material that supports it. Here, for example, is the synopsis of Chapter 1 of a proposed book on seafaring:

> 1. First Ventures
>
> No one knows when humans first ventured on the water. They must have tried a tree trunk first, to cross a narrow stream or traverse a small lake. Soon people fashioned crude rafts by lashing together trees with fibers, just as aboriginal Tasmanians did as recently as the eighteenth century A.D. The dugout canoe, the first actual boat, may have developed from a hollow tree found floating, then taken over as a simple boat—the technology to hollow out logs is nothing more than a shell or stone axe and adze and skilled use of fire. I believe that the first watercraft developed in warmer waters, where people spent much of their life in shallows collecting mollusks and spearing fish. (Fagan, unpublished MS.)

In one paragraph, we've learned that no one knows when humans first went afloat, that rafts and dugouts were the earliest watercraft, and that they probably developed in warmer environments. Chapter 1 is background for the narrative chapters that follow.

Chapter Titles

Catchy titles sometimes work, but they should reflect the subject matter that follows. For example, Chapter 1 of the *Fish on Friday* outline was called "A Subsistence Diet," for it was concerned with diet and Western history. Much depends on your writing style, but avoid trendy titles or humor unless they accurately reflect the chapter's contents. Quotes sometimes work, but should be used carefully as epigraphs and communicate the subject matter.

Book Structure

In their invaluable book on publishing and writing, *Thinking Like Your Editor* (2002), Susan Rabiner and Alfred Fortunato stress the importance of the organizational structure of the book. They distinguish between three types of chapters: "context or background chapters; chapters that further the argument and narrative of the book; and break-narrative chapters" (Rabiner and Fortunato 2002:101). The context chapters discuss the topic and its controversies, or what they call "tensions," and set the stage. Argument and narrative chapters are where you develop your unique idea. Break-narrative chapters give the reader a rest from the narrative, are often more reflective, and can take a wider perspective than narrative ones. They set the general context for the chapters that follow. For instance, in *Fish on Friday*, I had to say something about medieval fishing methods, an obscure subject but obviously of central importance to my story. So I added a break-narrative chapter to my original outline:

> Chapter 3: Medieval Fishers
> Chapter 3 surveys the state of European fishing in the tenth century at the time when the shortage began. I will describe the differences between coastal fishing and fishing on lakes and rivers; fishmongers and fish markets; actual medieval fish recipes; fairs and the seasonal demand for fish; as well as concerns about overfishing in inland waters. This material will be introduced here both for its intrinsic interest and to foreshadow a later discussion of how these methods would be forced to change in response to new pressures—religious, societal, and climatic. The chapter ends by showing how limited was

the capability of the then existing fishing industry to meet the new demands being placed on it, and by describing the interest of the rising merchant class in exploiting the increasing demand for fish. (Fagan, unpublished MS.)

Placing the break narrative in Chapter 3 worked well in the proposal outline, but in the final manuscript the break narrative became parts of other chapters. The narrative flow worked better that way.

Distinguishing between these three chapter types and working out where they will go in the book will provide the structure for your outline.

Number of Chapters

This can vary from the twenty-three or so of a full-length, comprehensive textbook to the eight to twelve in a trade work. Unless you are writing a long book, I would aim, at any rate initially, for at most ten chapters, plus an introduction and epilogue. The exact number is bound to change as you write the book and as you consult with your editor.

Should the chapters be long or short? Much depends on the length of the book and the subject matter. A regional synthesis, like my *Ancient North America: The Archaeology of a Continent* (2004a) or Michael Moseley's *The Incas and Their Ancestors: The Archaeology of Peru* (2001), tends to have longer chapters in the 6,000-word-plus range. Textbook chapters can be up to 12,000 words or more, given the complexity of the subject matter and the amount of detail. Shorter books, like volumes in the well-known Archaeologist's Toolkit series, or, indeed, this volume, work best with shorter chapters. Short, punchy, and to the point, they carry the reader from one topic to the next in logical order. The average length of the chapters in this book is around 5,000 words.

In the case of *Fish on Friday*, the provisional outline called for twelve chapters. We ended up with seventeen, because the approach I took when actually writing it worked best with shorter chapters. The subject matter was at one moment ecclesiastical, at another concerned with fisheries, at a third with seafaring and explorers, so it made more sense to cut the narrative into smaller chunks, taking care to execute smooth chapter transitions.

Progression

Think about the sequence of chapters. Does the reader progress through the book? Is there an organizational spine? In many archaeological books the stepping-stones will be chronological. This works well for readers who are used to starting with the earliest and ending up with the most recent. There are, of course, other options. In my book *Chaco Canyon: Archaeologists Explore the Lives of an Ancient Society* (2005), I used a chronological gradient throughout the book, but varied it when discussing the earliest human occupation of the canyon. In Chapter 3, "Ultimate Ancestry," I worked my way back from A.D. 400 to first settlement, starting with the Basketmaker predecessors of the Ancestral Pueblo and ending with the Paleoindians. I wanted to work back in time to stress the deep cultural roots of the later Chacoans, for the qualities of these early foragers—flexibility, mobility, and opportunism—served their successors well. In writing his brilliant analysis of cave art, *The Mind in the Cave: Consciousness and the Origins of Art* (2002), David Lewis-Williams started with the discovery of human antiquity and the search for the meaning of the cave art. He used two case studies on southern African and North American rock art as the basis for much of his discussion of ancient shamanism. Three short "time-bytes," brief hypothetical scenarios at the beginning of the book, set the stage for his discussion and added dramatic tension. Everything depends on the subject matter and the kind of narrative you are developing.

Decide what information you have to introduce before the reader can begin the narrative. You'll move paragraphs and sentences around, shifting material into break-narrative chapters, and so on.

Once you have what you consider a viable outline, set it aside for a few days before revising it. Then set it aside once more before revising yet again. As part of the editing, check the outline against the narrative to find the inevitable inconsistencies. At this point, unless something about the outline makes you want to start again, it's probably ready for submission.

In Chapter 5, we complete the proposal process by discussing the specimen chapter and the important relationships that will shape your book.

CHAPTERS, EDITORS, AND AGENTS

Rule 5: Develop a good relationship with your editor.

"**YOU DON'T UNDERSTAND!** Writing is all about relationships," an experienced author once told me, when I complained about my solitary existence as a writer. Over the years, I've discovered how right he was. This chapter moves on from the narrative and provisional outline to writing specimen chapters. But we also discuss the important business and personal relationships that you forge with editors and agents as you develop your proposal.

Specimen Chapters

Some publishers require sample chapters, others do not. Much depends on your experience. A first-time author, even with an academic track record, should count on writing a chapter. In any case, it's a useful exercise.

Most general archaeology books involve narratives, so it's best to draft a chapter from the earlier part of the book. This saves prolonged explanations as to who is doing what to whom. Remember that you are writing a book that serves its readers, not an audience of fellow specialists. Again, think passion! Seduce the reader with a compelling narrative and a satisfying outcome. By all means quote (sparingly) from basic sources, introduce your interpretations, and, above all, avoid too much detail.

Here's an example from my book *Chaco Canyon*:

By A.D. 800, Chacoans lived in small structures that housed one to four households, permanent settlements of small-room suites, mostly on the south side of the canyon. They farmed the most fertile soils with simple methods refined over many centuries of experiment and experience. As we have seen, the ensuing decades were times of movement when people from the north moved into the canyon and settled there. I found mention in the literature of one founding community at Pueblo Pintado that used clay vessels with clear northern ties, which tends to confirm that at least some of the immigrants came from the north, others from the south. The process was probably amicable, involving arrangements with fellow kin who already lived at Chaco. During the next century, the canyon emerged as a major center of Pueblo society. This was also the time when the first great houses rose along the north wall and south side.

The immigrants brought new architectural ideas with them. We've seen how arc-shaped structures already flourished in the northern and southern San Juan by the ninth century. The prototypes of what we may safely call "great houses" existed elsewhere by the early 900s, in places where Chacoan outliers later came into being. Chaco itself was not yet the center of the San Juan world, its nascent great houses still relatively insignificant structures. Over the next two centuries, the canyon became an axis mundi, a major hub of the northern Southwest. Its great houses assumed a great complexity and prominence.

The great French historian Le Roy Ladurie once remarked that there were two kinds of historians, parachutists and truffle hunters. The parachutist observes the past from afar, on a grand scale, while the truffle hunter, fascinated by treasures in the soil, keeps a nose close to the ground. How right he is, and how well his comment also applies to archaeologists! Some of us are by temperament parachutists in everyday life. Many others are truffle hunters, with a fine mind for detail. I'm very much a parachutist, with a profound admiration for people who spend their careers studying the minute details of the past. I could never carry off the meticulous, time-consuming research involved with deciphering Chaco's great houses and the lives of the people who built them. This is some of the most complicated archaeology in the world. Archaeologists like Dabney Ford and Tom Windes spend their days in intricate detective work, poring over generations-old field notes, navigating through a maze of demolished and remodeled kivas, rooms, terraces, and plazas, through the ruins of structures that were never the same one year to the next. (Fagan 2005: 112–113)

Notice how I combined narrative with some background on the science, the broader picture with the narrow. I describe small-room suites, stress that agricultural methods were simple, and introduce the concept of movement, so central to Chaco's history. After introducing architectural innovations, I then use Le Roy Ladurie to introduce the complicated research needed to decipher Chaco great houses. This sets the stage for the real meat of the chapter, which unravels the history of the pueblos.

Some general books are argument-based, dealing with new ideas—for example, a fresh theory surrounding agricultural origins. Here the challenge is to present your ideas while being respectful to other approaches, and to take only a small part of your argument as the sample. In Chapter 5 of *Thinking Like an Editor* (2002), Rabiner and Fortunato have an excellent discussion of how to handle this kind of specimen chapter. They stress that your objective should not be to win the argument, for that will result in a one-sided book. Aggressive advocacy belongs on newspaper op-ed pages and on confrontational political shows on TV. The name of your game is reasoned analysis, and there are rules.

Write a defensible argument that makes you feel good about yourself, whatever the critics say.

Be sure to submit a highly polished sample, be it a complete chapter or part of one. This shows that you are a professional and competent writer, not a good academic—that's a given.

SOME RULES FOR REASONED ARGUMENT

■ Make the best case you can for the other side's position, with integrity and respect.

■ Set reasonable standards against which to evaluate your argument.

■ Do not lead others to believe something that is untrue.

■ Establish your basic givens solidly before you build on them.

■ Anticipate all possible alternative interpretations for all your data.

■ Assume that your audience will include those who agree and those who disagree with you, as well as others who are still neutral. This undecided group is your primary audience.

Finally . . . Read through Everything

When you've convinced yourself that you're finished, you're not! This is where you call, once again, on your long-suffering friends. Their dispassionate reading is bound to spot an inconsistency or two, even a howler, like the time when I spelled "Mississippian" three different ways in a proposal narrative. Once you have their comments, revise the proposal one last time. Now, you're finally ready to submit it to editors at one or more publishing houses.

That All-Important Person—the Editor

Serious writing depends heavily on the quality of the relationships you forge in the process. Some of my closest friends are editors and others in the publishing business. We've developed a profound level of trust in personal and professional relationships that helps us produce good books together. The quality of the partnerships you enjoy during your writing career is of fundamental importance in a publishing world where there are already too many books and a bottom-line mentality that rewards quantity over quality. Archaeology, for all its diversity, is still a comparative village in professional and social terms. But the world of books is a huge city with myriad, crowded neighborhoods where the quality of your contacts and relationships is of paramount importance.

There's a complicated typology of editors in publishing, at least some of whom you'll encounter during the life of your book.

Here we're concerned with the sponsoring editor, referred to hereafter simply as "the editor." Editors are the most important people in your writing life. They have a difficult job, mediating as they do between the pressures of the commercial market, their bottom-line-obsessed lords and mistresses, and the writer, often thousands of miles away. I've worked with dozens of editors over the years—superb, prosaic, and truly appalling. I've learned that a long-term relationship with a truly outstanding, caring editor is one of the most rewarding professional marriages you can experience.

Time was when editors stayed at the same house for most of their careers, cherished their authors, and edited every line of their manuscripts. Many of them worked with the same authors on book after book, nurturing their talents and developing their careers. Alas, such editors are a dying breed in both the text and trade business, partly because of the prevalence of agents in trade publishing, who now oversee their writers' careers, and also because of the sheer pressure of work thrust upon editorial shoulders. Many editors I know are shepherding eight or nine books through final manuscript stage at once, this quite apart from acquiring new ones. Line-editing is often cursory, sometimes lacking altogether.

If ever there was an instance where relationships are everything, it is when writing books. If you sign a contract with a really good, caring editor, who will line-edit meticulously, stand behind your book, become your advocate with the publisher, and, above all, think of you as a long-term investment, you should never work with anyone else again. Such relationships soon become trusting partnerships, where editor and author unite in a common goal—to produce an absolutely

A Typology of Editors

- Sponsoring editors, often just called "editors," commission books and nurture them through to publication and beyond.

- Acquisition editors acquire books, then hand them over to others once the contract is signed.

- Development editors work on textbooks (not trade books) to ensure that they conform to market norms and cover the correct material. They also work on draft manuscripts before copyediting.

- Art editors are responsible for illustration programs on more elaborate books, especially coffee-table volumes.

- Production editors supervise the design and production of your book after it has been approved by editorial.

- Copy editors edit your manuscript for style, house rules, and consistency.

first-rate product. From your point of view, it means that the editor is no longer judging your ability as a writer, but working with you to solve problems as the manuscript evolves.

I've been lucky and developed close relationships with several text and trade editors, where they literally become an extension of the family. You learn to trust their judgment and can ask freely for advice. Some years ago, as I worked on my book on El Niños (Fagan 1999), I reached the last chapter and could not get it right. I read it and reread it, knowing that something was missing. In despair, I e-mailed it to New York. A few days later, my editor sent it back. "This may work," he wrote. All he had done was add a fifty-word paragraph about two-thirds of the way through the chapter and everything fell into place.

If you are fortunate in your editor and your first book works well, you'll find yourself discussing potential future projects even as you're still writing your current work. This is a fascinating sort of interchange, which often leads to nothing but sometimes produces an intriguing idea. Your editor knows the ever-changing marketplace in ways you do not, as many subjects cross the editorial desk. Editors discern market niches and potentially important subjects, and generate ideas that never would have occurred to you. When proposal time comes, they'll suggest revisions and then fight for your project before their editorial board.

There are writers who advocate taking their ideas wherever they can receive more money up-front. They hop from one publisher to another and never settle down. Wrong! Find a really good editor and cherish the relationship. In the long run, you'll make just as much money, if not more if the book takes off.

Beware of acquisitions editors, whose job is to search for new titles. They'll sign your book, but when the manuscript arrives in-house, it'll be assigned elsewhere. You'll have no in-house mentor for your work. Go with an editor who stays with your book until it appears and becomes its marketing advocate. In that way, you have continuity, a confidant, and someone who is there for you if you have a problem with the book, have to postpone delivery for a family emergency, and so on.

The editorial relationship, even if you have an agent, is the most important one of all.

To Agent or Not to Agent

Literary agents come into play in the general trade market. As a rule, textbook contracts do not require an agent, as they are boilerplate documents. Nor do agreements with university presses, unless you're writing a general trade book for them. Books with potentially limited markets involve small sums of money and do not interest most agents. At the major trade houses, however—for example, Knopf or Random House—the editors will usually only accept proposals from agents. Unsolicited manuscripts go into the slush pile, which is either skimmed quickly by junior staff members or just ignored. There are, of course, stories of best sellers that emerged by chance from the slush pile, but most of them are apocryphal. Unless you have a brilliant idea and a personal contact with an editor (who will probably recommend a list of agents), you work with ideas and proposals through the agent, who becomes the intermediary between author and editor until the book is signed.

WHAT AN AGENT DOES

- Acts as a talent scout for large publishing houses: you have the benefit of your agent's network.

- Helps you develop ideas and a proposal from there. A good agent will insist that a proposal be revised again and again until he or she feels it has a good chance of acceptance.

- Sends out your proposal to selected editors who might be interested in the idea. Unless you are working regularly with the same editor (as is usually the case for me), or your contract with your existing publisher has a first-refusal clause, your proposal will go to several places.

- Receives any offers for your book and conducts an auction between competing houses if such a competitive situation develops. I once sat in an agent's office and heard him field a series of calls that took an advance for a book up from $100,000 to $250,000 in minutes. This, unfortunately, was not one of my books!

- Negotiates the contract with the publisher—not only advances, schedules of payments, royalty rates, and so on, but such details as first rights of refusal on future books and other potential minefields.

- Receives all payments from the publisher, checks royalty statements, and sends you out the resulting funds, less commission. As part of this service, the agent also issues tax documents.

■ Deals with problems when they arise. If, for example, you need a contract deadline change, or otherwise run into trouble, he or she will negotiate on your behalf with the publisher. Perhaps your publisher goes out of business, sells their list, or cancels dozens of contracts. This is when your agent is essential. You may never need this kind of help, but when you do, you'll be thankful for an agent with a tough-minded approach.

■ Arranges reversion of rights to you when a book goes out of print.

Good agents are wonderful assets, who work hard for their clients. They generally take a 15 percent commission off all advances and royalties for their services and are well worth it if substantial sums of money are involved. My agent is a mixture of a friend, a business manager, an advocate, and a no-nonsense critic.

Finding an agent is hard, especially for first-time authors without a track record. Most good agents are not actively looking for clients, but will sometimes consider an over-the-transom approach. To get their attention, you'll need a short document that really sells your idea in the first paragraph. That means an eye-catching idea, a passionate style, and a clear vision of your story. Treat selling yourself to an agent like selling to a publisher's editor. Even then, you may be unlucky, but a good agent is always on the lookout for exciting ideas.

There are agents who specialize in professorial clients, often referred by other academic writers. The Web has plenty of listings that will guide you, among them www.writers-free-reference.com/agents and www.writers.net/agents.html. Don't become involved with an agent who wants to charge you a fee for reading your manuscript. Most of them won't produce a contract for you, for they make their money off reading your proposal. As with anything on the Web, exercise caution.

As with editors, a good agent relationship is a priceless asset. A good agent is a powerful ally and should be cherished. But you're unlikely to need an agent for most trade books for the archaeology niche. If you don't have an agent, you can always consult a lawyer who specializes in intellectual property about your proposed contract.

Contracts

As I've stressed, successful general writing is at least partially, and sometimes wholly, a commercial enterprise, so part of the publisher relationship in your life is financial.

Most archaeologists live off grants or CRM contracts. Someone who writes a general work, a text, or a mass-market book will never receive a grant like those awarded for specialist research. The only exception is when a book is commissioned by a society or some other organization, which raises the money for you to write a general synthesis of their work. This has happened to me only twice in my career. Almost invariably, the only money for the research and writing of your book is going to come from the publisher in the form of an advance on royalties.

Authors are paid by royalties, a sliding-scale percentage of (commonly) the net price of the book. Typically, a publisher pays royalties every six months, often on April 1 and October 1, so this is a lump-sum business, whether your book is an international best seller or a synthesis of the archaeology of a small region of the Southwest. While many academic books are published without advances against royalties and often never pay royalties at all on tiny sales, general works usually make a small amount of money and occasionally considerable sums.

An advance against royalties is just that—a loan from the publisher that is earned back by future sales. The house gambles on potential sales and factors in the amount of the advance as the book is approved for signing. There is no such thing as an average advance. Some are little more than a couple of thousand dollars, usually for niche books or reprints. Advances in the $10,000 to $20,000 range are not uncommon, especially for books on popular subjects like ancient Egypt, where larger sales are virtually guaranteed. Above $20,000, you enter the realm of agents, major books, and stellar ideas or discoveries. An advance in the middle five figures is rare for archaeological subjects, and $100,000 and above is almost unheard of—it would require a book that sold at least 30,000 copies in hardcover, probably more. In short, you are not going to get rich, and even if you get a $20,000 advance, your research expenses, especially travel, will eat up a great deal of it.

Textbook advances tend to be modest, except for the enormous, intensely competitive mass-market introductory books in psychology, English, and perhaps biological anthropology. Even then, low five-figure advances are relatively rare. Do not believe those who tell you that some archaeologists receive multimillion-dollar advances! They do not, and even high five-figure advances are sometimes contingent on achieving hardcover sales goals.

Advances are typically paid half on signing, half on delivery. Sometimes you will receive a third on signing, a third on completion, and a third on publication, which spreads out the money.

If your book does not earn back your advance, the publisher absorbs the loss. Although technically you are liable for the unearned portion, in practice you'll never be asked to pay it back. If, however, you either fail to deliver a manuscript or write an unacceptable one, publishers are entirely within their rights to demand their money back—and they will. This is where agents are invaluable, especially if considerable sums are involved. It's wise to think of an advance as a loan until your book is accepted and in production.

While most publishers pay royalties, some organizations, notably the National Geographic Society and book packagers (publishers who assemble books, then market the package to another publisher), pay you a lump sum for your work. You surrender all rights, receive no royalties, and are treated as an independent contractor doing a work for hire. You receive the lump sum for your text in stages, according to progress made. With this type of contract, you never receive anything extra if the book sells exceptionally well, but it's prestigious to publish with National Geographic and they are quite generous with their stipends, as they are with obtaining illustrations and other matters. You have to be prepared to write the book in short order, maybe a few months, and to deliver on time.

Publishing contracts can be complex, highly varied documents, especially in the general trade market, where you need an agent to guide you through the intricacies of such issues as foreign and TV rights. You may receive a contract that entitles the publisher to negotiate foreign rights, which is probably the best way to go. In some cases, your agent will sell only the domestic rights and retain the foreign rights for independent sale. You'll never make large sums from foreign rights, but it's fascinating to receive your book in, say, Japanese, where you cannot read a word except your name. In some cases, payments from foreign publishers trickle on for years. I am still receiving royalties from the Italian edition of *The Rape of the Nile*, published in 1975. The last statement paid me $15.72. One day, I know I'll get a check for ten cents!

The financial side of writing can become complex, especially if you write several textbooks that go into multiple editions. You need to develop a close relationship with your accountant as far as taxes are concerned. And, please, have no illusions: only a handful of authors make a living off freelance writing about archaeology, and all of them have been at it a long time.

Once you have signed your contract, it's time to start work on the first draft, the subject of Chapter 6.

WRITING THE FIRST DRAFT

Rule 6: Make writing a daily habit.

T HE MOMENT YOU GENERATE sentences that might appear in your
completed account, you have begun your writing," writes Harry
Wolcott in *Writing Up Qualitative Research* (2001:13). Writing
the first draft is the most daunting moment of the entire enterprise.
You sit at the computer and contemplate a blank space. Inevitably,
thoughts of the thousands of words that lie ahead cross your mind.
How do you start? What should you do to ensure that the first draft
progresses steadily?

Writing as a Habit

I walked upstream along the floor of the great canyon as the cool of
evening settled over Chaco. The sun cast the steep cliffs in deep relief. Pueblo Bonito's weathered ruins glowed with a roseate orange as
massing clouds towered high above, dwarfing outcrop and site alike.
As the shadows lengthened, I gazed upward at the wide bowl of the
heavens and imagined the canyon nine hundred years ago. A chill wind
sloughed at my back as I sat down to enjoy the spectacular sunset.

Chaco came alive; I sensed the acrid scent of wood smoke carried on the evening breeze, dogs barking at the setting sun. Flickering hearths and blazing firebrands highlight dark windows and doorways on the terraces of the great house that is Pueblo Bonito. People move between light and shadow, dark silhouettes against the flames. The shrill cries of children playing in the shadows, the quiet talk of men leaning against sun-baked walls—the past comes alive in the gloaming. So does the most pervasive sound of all: the scrape, scrape of dozens of grinders against dozens of milling stones as the women prepare the evening meal. (Fagan 2005:3)

These are the initial words of an 80,000-word book on Chaco Canyon. They ushered in the writing of a first draft that took just over three months to set down. The published words you just read bear little resemblance to what I wrote that first day. I vividly remember starting work on the book. It was a spring morning, a beautiful day when I should have been out sailing. Instead, I was looking at an empty window on my computer and cursing the day that I became a writer. It was then that I recited one of my mantras, the rule that heads this chapter: make writing a daily habit. I knew perfectly well that I couldn't go sailing until I had finished my day's stint at my desk. So I just started typing, letting the ideas flow. Three hours later, the wind was filling in nicely from the west and I was on the water with an easy conscience.

Whenever I speak to literary groups or at writers' conferences, the inevitable question always crops up: how do you write? What is your work routine? Almost invariably there's a frisson of disappointment when I start talking about writing as a habit that has obligations to a publisher. Many in the audience believe that a writer's life is filled with creative moments, when fire from heaven descends on your head and you turn out inspired prose. Yes, there is inspiration involved in writing, sometimes even genius, and there are those writers with powerful egos who love talking about the "writerly craft" and "solitary contemplation," but almost invariably they are using mystique to sell books. The fact is that writing is a hard slog along the way, word after word, sentence after sentence, paragraph after paragraph. You've got to get words on paper. Even if you are writing a book as part of a busy life consulting, teaching, or doing basic research, the only way you will complete a manuscript within a reasonable time is to set an immutable routine for your writing.

Most writers I've talked to say that the most they can achieve in a day is about four hours of original writing. After that the quality drops off, so they turn to other tasks or simply stop work. The four-hour figure is just an estimate. I know some writers who work at it eight hours a day. I know others who are exhausted after two. It doesn't matter, provided you're happy with your routine.

Before you write a word, establish a schedule and keep to it. Sit down with your calendar and look at the pattern of appointments, family commitments, and so on. Very quickly, you'll establish a time during the day when you can guarantee a minimum of two hours of uninterrupted time. Then schedule it as an immutable engagement that can be broken by nothing short of illness or a serious family emergency. Tell your family and your colleagues that you are not available during these hours. The first day you set the schedule, shut the door, switch off or ignore the phone, resist the temptation to look at e-mail, and just write.

Sounds easy, doesn't it? Actually it is, once you've established the habit and have kept to it for a couple of weeks. It's like working out regularly. After a while, the routine becomes second nature and you look forward to the solitary hours of uninterrupted writing.

Procrastination is not an option when you are working on a contractual deadline on what is, ultimately, a commercial enterprise with sometimes considerable sums of money involved. Remember that any advance from the publisher is a loan against future earnings. This means that the deadlines in your contract are, in effect, loan due dates. The sooner you set up a plan for paying off the loan, the better. It helps a great deal, too, if you have a comfortable work space.

Work Space

I've written in libraries, on trains, on planes high above the Pacific, in tented camps, on cruise ships, aboard small yachts, even in the toilet. But, ultimately, I come back, cocoonlike, to my home office.

Your needs should be simple but discerning, sufficient to allow you to write for long periods of time. Many people use their work office, or migrate to the peace and quiet of a library, but I have always found working at home less distracting. My home office is a delight, a 1930s-style garage that is now a quiet workplace with north-facing windows and a Dutch door that opens out on the garden. My books and files are a few steps away; the computer, scanner, and printer are set up just the way I want. I have a second large table, where I can work with yellow pad and pencil in longhand, a useful trick when the going is tough or the argument a complicated one. An ergonomic swivel chair allows me to swing from one table to the other in a moment.

My office is my nest where I can contemplate, read, even take a nap, and a place where I can leave things spread out overnight—if the cats haven't annexed my research notes as a couch. In that case, I risk my life to move them gently elsewhere. (A resident cat is a lovely piece of reassuring furniture, except when he or she decides to stroll over your keyboard or settle in your lap expecting caresses.) If I need coffee, tea, a snack, or alcohol, the kitchen is ten feet away; the back door is close by if UPS calls.

"Pamper yourself," says Harry Wolcott, and he is right, urging that we recognize our individual idiosyncrasies. What will help you sit down and write, and keep you working day after day? Is it background music? Provide it. A resident cat? Acquire one. A coffee pot always perking? Make sure it's close by. Provided these minor indulgences don't become distractions, they're powerful incentives to get to work. Some people like an austere, monastic writing environment, others prefer to wallow in comfort with every need at hand. I'm somewhere between the two extremes. Live with your work space, then change it around until you're completely satisfied. You'll minimize logistical distractions this way.

A computer is, of course, your best friend. By this stage I'm totally computer dependent, although I'm an idiot at the technicalities. Whatever you use, be sure that you have enough memory and a good backup system. Have you ever lost a final draft in a computer crash without a backup? I once lost a 75,000-word manuscript that way. Fortunately I had a previous version in hard copy. I won't make that mistake again. Get a serious printer, preferably a high-volume laser printer that prints fast in black-and-white. Your computer equipment will be your largest investment. Choose it carefully, learn the basics you need, and start writing. Today, with laptops so powerful, I now use an Apple MacBook Pro attached to a 30-inch monitor, so I can, if need be, take the computer on a trip.

Word-processing programs are legion, but the one most commonly used by publishers is Microsoft Word, so you're probably best off using that, for all its faults.

Getting Started

Write! Write! The mantra slips easily off the tongue, but getting started is never easy. It may take you a while to get started each day. Some writers brew coffee first, others sharpen pencils or even do the ironing. Many of us sit down automatically in front of the computer, where we procrastinate with e-mail, the new enemy, especially if your computer tells you if you have an incoming message. The temptation to take a look is almost overpowering. I now discipline myself to check e-mail at fixed times, about every two hours. Before I start writing, I deal with the messages that have come in overnight, so that I start with a clean slate.

The blank computer screen haunts us. How do we move ahead from here? The answer may seem ridiculously cold-blooded, but it works. Set an allocation of a fixed number of words a day, not finishing work until you have them. Do not go back and revise, just concentrate on getting words written. Your instincts may tell you that you are writing garbage, or superb stuff. Ignore them and just keep writing. At the revision stage you will probably sling out at least half the original text, but that's not the point. You've got a rough manuscript on paper and gotten over the psychological hump of writing the first draft.

How many words should you plan on writing daily? Some people write slowly, agonizing over each word even at first-draft stage. Others, like me, press on, knowing that numerous revisions will settle matters of organization and style. A common goal, which I share with many authors, is to write 1,000 words a day. This seems like a lot until you realize that it's only about four double-spaced typescript pages. But think about it for a moment: if you write 1,000 words a day, Monday through Friday, that's 5,000 words, just short of the average chapter length. Multiply that by four and you have 20,000 words in a month, a good quarter of the words in a typical trade book. The mathematics makes the point. Write 1,000 words a day and you'll complete your first draft within four months.

Try a target of 1,000 words daily for a week or so, then scale back or add more if you feel more comfortable with a different figure. You'll be surprised how easily you settle into a routine, but be prepared for good days and bad. The symptoms of a bad day hit hard—misspellings, sentences that don't form themselves easily, uncertainty as to how to embark on a project, then yawns and stretches. You brew coffee, consult the word count every few minutes, and watch the total slowly creep up to the target number. Eventually it does, and you thankfully move on with your day. Fortunately, the words come easier most of the time. You'll learn from experience roughly how many hours a day you need to complete your allocation and set your routine accordingly. Then there are those all-too-rare magical days when your fingers dance over the keyboard and the words pour out effortlessly. Before you know what's going on, you've written 2,000 words, even more. I haven't had one of those days for months, but when I do, it'll be memorable.

Whether it's a good day or bad day, keep going. Insist that you complete the allocation before you shut down the computer. Occasionally, you're bound to miss a day for the soundest of reasons. Don't fret. Try to add 100 words a day for the next few days to catch up. Do take at least one day a week off to allow your mind to relax. Within reason, don't worry about the prose you're writing. Just get the words on paper for later revision and make sure the narrative is well researched and accurate. Then, when you've finished your daily ration, spend any spare writing time during the rest of the day on the research for tomorrow's writing.

The name of the game is habit.

Procrastination and Writer's Block

Some time ago, I had a bad attack of writer's block. A chapter of *Fish on Friday* dealing with English voyages to North America was giving me trouble. The editor wanted major changes, and I was nervous about them. I sat in front of the computer with my draft text and his comments and couldn't get started. What triggered my procrastination, I don't know, but I suspect it was the fear of getting it wrong and having the chapter thrown back at me yet again.

I used any excuse not to work on the chapter. A book review was due against a tight deadline. I wrote it. Some proofs needed correction. I dealt with them. But *Fish on Friday* was due in New York in a few weeks and I knew I had to get on with it, like it or not. In the end, I made myself use the 1,000 word routine, rewriting the chapter as a flow of consciousness, using my research and the editor's comments as a guide. The strategy worked. Within a few days, the procrastination was just a memory and the editor was pleased with the revision.

Every author, however experienced, confronts writer's block. It's like having a cold. There are famous instances of novelists who have written nothing for years, seemingly burdened by procrastination, often a feeling of inadequacy and a fear of failure. The English novelist E. M. Forster was famous for his writer's block, which drove his publisher (who happened to be my father) to distraction. He wouldn't write a word for weeks, would not answer letters, and suffered from insomnia. The novelist Cormac McCarthy, believed by many literati to be America's greatest writer since Faulkner and Hemingway, published a new novel after seven years. *No Country for Old Men* (2005) was hailed as "an event" by reviewers; the author took a long time to complete this beautifully written, violent work. Fortunately, most authors suffer from the disease only sporadically and develop strategies for dealing with it. It's easier to overcome writer's block when writing archaeology or other nonfiction, where you deal with fewer intangibles.

We all have our strategies. One author I know plays Wagner for hours on end and forces herself into an "epic" frame of mind that positively drives her to write. She's a novelist with heroic leanings, so Wagner works for her. Another friend, a runner, ups his running schedule until the block evaporates. He works out his writing problem as he runs. There are those who eat cookies, go on a diet of black coffee, and a few who simply give up and wait for a trigger to set them writing again.

Time was when I was paralyzed by writer's block for weeks on end. I would struggle to set even a few words on paper, usually because I was intimidated by the size of the project, or because I feared the reaction of academic colleagues. Fortunately, experience has taught me the telltale symptoms—lassitude, a lack of enthusiasm for the subject, no passionate desire to write. These normally surface in the middle of a first draft, when the end is nowhere in sight. When I sense a pending attack, I use several proven strategies:

- **Change subjects.** For me, the fatal thing is to stop writing, so I move away from the task at hand and tackle some other job that's on the pile instead: reviews, short articles, book reports for publishers, and so on. The change of subject matter often gives me renewed energy and a hunger to get back to the main job.

- **Persist.** I force myself to write my 1,000 words a day. The first two or three days are hellishly slow, with temptations to quit at every turn. Then suddenly the tide changes. I find myself engrossed in new evidence, entranced by the prospects of a subplot in my narrative, or simply having a good day at the keyboard.

- **Get a colleague to help.** Some years ago, I had a nasty block over the Ancestral Pueblo out-migration from Chaco Canyon. I suspected the problem was fear of criticism from colleagues. So I flew over to Tucson. A friend there introduced me to Gwinn Vivian, one of the leading authorities on Chaco. I walked him through my scenario, and he assured me I was on the right track. Back home, the words flowed out of me.

Whatever you do, don't sit back helplessly complaining. That will get you nowhere.

Research

By the time you've written your preliminary document, you'll have a pretty good idea of the literature for each chapter. With the first draft, you have to carry the research much further. There are four basic sources of information.

The Literature

When you are writing an academic monograph, you read everything relevant in the specialist literature. Researching a general book re-

Four Sources of Information When Researching

■ The academic literature and more general works.

■ Material acquired during interviews with researchers and colleagues.

■ Insights from museum collections and site visits.

■ Your personal experience.

quires another strategy. You need an entirely different mind-set, where you make hard-nosed judgments as to the relevance of the literature.

Professor Grahame Clark of Cambridge University was an authoritative synthesizer of archaeological literature. Clark was an austere man with little patience for trivia and a mind-set focused on the wider picture, which was why he wrote *World Prehistory* (1961), the first truly global prehistory of humankind. I once asked him how he mastered so much literature. With books, he was forthright: "Peruse the table of contents, then read the final chapter. After that just read selectively if you think you need to." With papers, he was similarly ruthless: "Read the abstract, then the conclusions. You'll find out quickly if it's relevant or significant." At the time, I had no intention of writing a popular book on archaeology, let alone a more technical synthesis, but then I got drawn into multidisciplinary African history, where the issues were enormous and some general writing urgently needed. I found myself adopting Clark's approach, which has served me well ever since.

This mind-set requires admitting at once that you cannot master all the literature. So you ask tough questions. What are the most authoritative general surveys? Are there key monographs and, in particular, case studies and examples that are relevant to your story? For example, no one writing about underwater archaeology can do so without reading the literature on the Uluburun shipwreck off southern Turkey. What are the major controversies and issues? Here you have to delve back into the earlier literature, then refine your ideas with a judicious look at more recent writings.

You'll find that there are a few key books and articles that will provide the background for your story—their bibliographies should cover nearly all the relevant specialist literature. Almost certainly some specialist will have come up with your idea in the past—it's up to you to find the reference. In the case of California archaeology, for example, I found that there were about a dozen major papers that covered the main controversies, most of them written within the past fifteen years. You have to be ruthless in rejecting the irrelevant, the unduly specialized, and the bad. You soon develop a keen instinct for quality. The task is smaller than you think. In these days of proliferating journals, Internet publication, and publish-or-perish, much of what appears in print is irrelevant for your purposes. Of course, there are instances when you may want to delve more deeply into the specialized literature, as I did, for example, during the writing of *Fish on Friday*, with the zooarchaeology of ancient cod bones on Norway's Lofoten Islands. It will be clear when you critique your first draft where you need richer material or further insights. Peer reviews by specialist colleagues are helpful when you have a draft in hand.

Interviews

Interviewing is an art learned early by journalists, but not something mastered during archaeological training. I've found that colleagues love to talk about their work, either face-to-face or by e-mail. Almost invariably, they are helpful and delighted that you're taking an interest in their often esoteric research. I vividly remember the delighted response from an Assyriologist at Oxford University when I queried him about Tigris River flood levels in 1000 B.C. "Somebody is interested in my work!" he wrote, and gave me invaluable information. Then there was the scholar from Princeton who translated a passage in medieval French for me—and the innumerable archaeologists who have shared data, insights, stratigraphic profiles, and so on.

What about unpublished material? All of us sit on unpublished data in one form or another, which is effectively inaccessible to anyone else. Sometimes, research will be "in press" and tied up in the inevitable publication lag. There is also the issue of the so-called grey literature, CRM reports that are written for a government agency or a private client that are often inaccessible to outsiders. Perhaps they are confidential or stored away and forgotten. In recent years the situation has improved somewhat, thanks to databases and repositories, but a great deal of nonacademic archaeology is difficult to access, especially to someone without specialist knowledge and the personal contacts that go with it. This was a major problem when I wrote *Ancient North America* (2004a), the archaeology of a continent where most archaeology is now written in CRM reports. Our knowledge of North American archaeology would be considerably different if all CRM literature were freely accessible. But it is not, so we work with what we can find. I was criticized for stating in the preface to *Ancient North America* that "grey literature contributed relatively little to this book" and that "This book is written from published sources only." I am unrepentant, for the essence of general writing about any subject is that your book be accurate and based on accessible sources. Effectively, you are confined to published material, unless you have permission from someone with unpublished data to use it, or you control the information yourself.

If a colleague shares such data with you, be sure to get specific permission to use it, and, if it is in any way elaborate, send him or her a draft of your text to review. In the case of the Skyrocket site in California mentioned in Chapter 1, Roger La Jeunesse and John Pryor reviewed what I wrote for *Before California: An Archaeologist Looks at Our Earliest Inhabitants* (2003) and contributed invaluable comments, which I ended up publishing in the notes and references section of the book. Make sure that you recognize such collegial assistance in your acknowledgments. And, if you quote a colleague, run the quote by him or her before it goes into print, and reference it as "personal communication" or "interview on (date)."

Apart from professional courtesy, scrupulous treatment of unpublished data and respect for "off the record" comments will gain you a reputation for integrity and straight dealing that may serve you well with future projects.

Museum Collections and Site Visits

Here common sense applies. Be scrupulous in obtaining permission to examine collections, and, on site, keep out of the way and don't take photographs without asking permission first. Once again, if you obey the rules and respect protocols, doors will open for you everywhere.

Personal Experience

> The waters of the Blackwater River in eastern England were pewter grey, riffled by an arctic northeasterly breeze. Thick snow clouds hovered over the North Sea. Heeling to the strengthening wind, we tacked down river with the ebb, muffled to our ears in every stitch of clothing we had aboard. *Braseis* coursed into the short waves of the estuary, throwing chill spray that froze as it hit the deck. Within minutes, the decks were sheathed with a thin layer of ice. (Fagan 2000:xi)

I will never forget that short April cruise when the weather was truly arctic. The memory brings chills even now. But the experience was a wonderful way to set the stage for *The Little Ice Age: How Climate Made History, 1300–1850*. All of us have rich personal experience to draw on, from archaeology and from life. Fiction writers draw heavily on their personal experience and with good reason—for etching in characters, adding color, and describing locations. There's absolutely no reason why you shouldn't use a memory, a vivid event, to bring your nonfiction narrative alive. I've used my sailing experience many times, as well as rich archaeological memories: Hadrian's Wall on a grey rainy day with the wind scudding clouds across the deserted ramparts; Chaco Canyon during and after a thunderstorm; Great Zimbabwe in Central Africa at full moon, to mention only a few such moments.

Outlines

You embark on the first draft with the provisional outline beside you, which is your blueprint for the book. Do you need a more detailed outline? Some authors spend weeks developing such documents based on their research notes; others prefer to forge right ahead with sheaves of notes at hand. This is entirely a matter of personal preference, but if you do use a detailed outline, beware of losing sight of the larger objectives in a mass of irrelevant detail. An outline does break down the book into manageable chunks, which need not necessarily be written in linear fashion. I, and indeed many authors, prefer to forge ahead without an outline, letting each chapter develop itself. Then, at revision stage, I outline the chapter on a yellow pad as a double-check.

Narrative Techniques

Archaeology is redolent with potential stories, be it the momentous consequences of the invention of the bone needle, the tale of the camel saddle, or the Ancestral Pueblo out-migration from Chaco Canyon. Let's look briefly at some techniques that can help build your narrative.

Chronological Gradient

Archaeologists are lucky in that they deal with cultural change through time. With nearly every idea you explore, there's some form of chronology, which you can use as the backbone for your story. For instance, if you write a world prehistory, you begin with human origins and end with the pre-industrial civilizations. In the case of Chaco Canyon, I told the story of the canyon's people starting with the Paleo-indians, then working forward in time. This gave the book an implicit spine—a signpost, as it were.

There are, of course, other ways of structuring a book. *In What This Awl Means: Feminist Archaeology at a Wahpeton Dakota Village* (1993), Janet Spector used a small antler handle of an iron awl used to perforate leather as the linchpin for her reconstruction of life at the Inyan Ceyaka Atonwan site in Minnesota. Her book tells the story of how the archaeologists collaborated with the Dakota Indian descendants of the people who lived at the settlement. She found out that the awl probably belonged to a woman named Mazaokiyewin and told her life story, including a scenario for the loss of the tool. Spector mediated between archaeology, oral tradition, and Native American relationships with their history. She describes her feelings afterward:

> I still find myself wishing for a time machine. I dream of spending just one day at Little Rapids with some members of our project . . . and some of the nineteenth century figures linked to Inyan Ceyaka Atonwan. . . . I can visualize the day, but it is difficult to picture how we would communicate given the distances between us. (Spector 1993:129)

Your approach to your story is limited only by your imagination.

Evocative Descriptions

In Chapter 4, we talked about narrative and break-narrative chapters. Evocative descriptions are a form of break narrative that you can use very effectively to set the stage for coming events, for a long description of a site, and, most important of all, to bring the readers into the narrative, so they feel they are there. Here's a short passage from *Cro-Magnon*, a book I wrote about the late Ice Age, which, among things, describes contacts between Neanderthals and modern humans:

> Four dots move along a riverbank in a black and gray Ice Age landscape of 40,000 years ago, the only sign of life on a cold, late autumn day. Dense morning mist swirls gently over the slow-moving water, stirring fitfully in an icy breeze. Pine trees crowd on the riverbank, close to a large clearing where aurochs and bison paw through the snow for fodder. The fur-clad Cro-Magnon family moves slowly—a hunter with a handful of spears, his wife carrying a leather bag of dried meat, a son and daughter. The five-year-old boy dashes to and fro brandishing a small spear. His older sister stays by her mother, also carrying a skin bag. A sudden gust lifts the clinging gloom on the far side of the stream. Suddenly, the boy shouts and points, then runs in terror to his mother. The children burst into tears and cling to her. A weathered, hirsute face with heavy brows stares out quietly from the undergrowth on the other bank. Expressionless, yet watchful, its Neanderthal owner stands motionless, seemingly oblivious to the cold. The father looks across, waves his spear and shrugs. The face vanishes as silently as it had appeared. (Fagan 2010b:ix)

Here we've imagined what it might have been like for a modern human family to encounter a Neanderthal in the heart of a chilly Ice Age landscape. Few words were involved, but they worked. This is where your personal experience of sites and terrain can come in. Use the weather, clouds, colors, anything that etched the scene in your mind. In that way you'll carry the reader with you and bring color to your narrative.

Reconstructions

Reconstructions are an effective way of introducing a subject, changing topics, and bringing a dry archaeological record to life—provided they are scientifically accurate.

Writing a convincing reconstruction requires firsthand knowledge of a location and of the archaeology. In *Before California*, I used a swordfish dancer to begin a chapter titled "The Realm of the Supernatural":

The dancer's headdress and cape shimmered in the firelight, a cascade of abalone shell fragments glittering down his back. He wore a swordfish skull complete with beak, which projected out from his forehead, the great eyes depicted in abalone fragments set in asphalt. Feathers and breast ornaments replicated the fins. The dancer mimicked the movements of the swordfish as it leaped from the water. Tonight, the swordfish is the ritual guest, honored for bringing ample whale meat to the people.

The pursuit of the swordfish in deep water involved risk and skill as well as prestige. Numerous Chumash myths identify the great fish as their marine allies, who drove whales ashore for humans to feed upon. Elaborate costumes, dances, and feasting honored this most formidable of prey, an equal in the complex world of his hunters. The swordfish were people. "They had a house at the bottom of the ocean, but there was no water inside." A fisherman once glimpsed one, a squat man. "On his head was a long bone, his instrument of attack. The fisherman threw a rock and the 'elye'wun jumped far out into the water and disappeared." (Fagan 2003:177)

I was careful to document the reconstruction in the notes and references section:

Chumash story quoted from T. C. Blackburn. *December's Child: A book of Chumash oral narratives* (Berkeley: University of California Press, 1975). Pp. 192–93. An account of swordfish rituals and a remarkable swordfish dancer's burial appears in D. Davenport, J. R. Johnson, and J. Timbrook. "The Chumash and the Swordfish." *Antiquity* 67 (1993): 257–72. (Fagan 2003:372)

For obvious reasons, I always get my reconstructions checked by a colleague. It's amazing what can slip by you. They are, of course, a central element in fiction of all kinds, including the famous Jean Auel Stone Age epics, beginning with *The Clan of the Cave Bear.*

Beware of the "Juan was a ten-year-old Maya boy. His father was a magnificent lord . . ." kind of reconstruction. They are very difficult to carry off convincingly and are best avoided, except, perhaps, in children's books, a genre unto its own.

Avoiding Undue Detail

Detail! We archaeologists love it. We tend to forget that others do not share our fascination. When writing a general narrative, be ruthless about eliminating unnecessary detail and anything that smacks of a list of artifacts or culture traits. We'll return to this point in Chapter 7.

There are occasional moments when arcane detail can be used as an effective tangent to the narrative. Ivor Nöel Hume's research on the gold thread from Martin's Hundred is one example that brought his story to life. Provided you don't use this trick too often, it can be effective.

Quotes

Quotes tend to be a disease in academic books. The infection spills over into general writing. Only use them when they are vital—for instance, a firsthand historical account of a site, if used judiciously, is effective. So is an apt or pithy remark, like P. G. Wodehouse's description of a construction site that could double for any excavation: "A mere hole in the ground, which of all sights is perhaps the least vivid and dramatic, is enough to grip their attention for hours at a time" (Wodehouse 1919:14).

The quote is a luxury to be used sparingly. Most of the time you can write it better yourself, especially if you are quoting academic writing.

Varying the Pace

Yes, Virginia, narratives can be dull, almost always because they are paced uniformly or overburdened with detail. Nothing is drearier than a catalog of obscure sites, chronologies, and artifacts, or a monotonal story that plods on and on. Use reconstructions, evocative descriptions, and other short diversions to vary the pace. Personal experiences also help vary things.

Brief tangents are a useful tool for pace changing. When I wrote a chapter on the changes wrought by acorns on ancient California society, I spent three pages describing balanophagy, the consumption of acorns, ancient and modern. Balanophagy was a nice diversion in a chapter that covered a great deal of archaeological ground. At the same time, it gave the reader a briefing on what acorns involve for the user, their advantages and disadvantages.

First-Person Writing

Sparing use of the first person works well. By sharing your reactions to artifacts, discoveries, sites, and incidents in your archaeological life, you bring a wonderful immediacy and often a sense of place to your writing, as the reader shares in the excitement, the passion, the evocative moment. Using your memories means drawing aside the veil of your personal life, but it's worth it. Use colors and the weather, the play of clouds on smooth water, the echoing sounds of a cathedral where stained glass reflects on the floor—anything is fair game provided it works, it's true, and it's accurate. You can write it as reminiscence or as a first-person narrative about memorable archaeologists you have met or who influenced you, or you can recount an experience where a site evoked powerful impressions. This happened to me at

Head-Smashed-In, the bison kill site in southern Alberta, Canada. Up in the shallow depression above the cliff where the bison gathered,

> I stumbled across the low stone cairns, scattered across the short grass in long, converging drive lines. . . . I imagined the dry brush set in them rustling and stirring in the wind on the day of the hunt so that they functioned for all the world like scarecrows. (Fagan 1985:61)

Personal experience can evoke powerful reactions in your readers and is a rich part of the romance of archaeology.

* * * *

After weeks of work, you'll come to the last chapter and that wonderful moment when you realize you have a complete first draft. Take a few days off and forget the book before tackling the all-important revisions that lie ahead.

REVISION, REVISION

Rule 7: Revision is the essence of good writing.
Listen to criticism and leave your ego at home.

But if we've become a supertanker among human societies, it's an oddly inattentive one. Only a tiny fraction of the people on board are engaging themselves with tending the engines. The rest are buying and selling goods among themselves, entertaining each other or studying the sky or the hydrodynamics of the hull. Those on the bridge have no charts or weather forecasts and cannot even agree that they are needed. . . . Few of those in command believe the gathering clouds have any relation to their fate or are concerned that there are lifeboats for only one in ten passengers. And no one dares to whisper in the helmsman's ear that he might consider turning the wheel. (Fagan 2004b:252)

THESE WORDS ARE PART of the last paragraph of *The Long Summer: How Climate Changed Civilization*, a book about ancient climate change, human adaptation, and, inevitably, anthropogenic global warming. I wrestled through several drafts of the closing chapter, a short epilogue to a book that covered such diverse societies as the

Sumerians, the Maya, and Tiwanaku. The first part of the chapter worked well, with a quote about the wrath of God and the day of reckoning, and then a discussion of the sense of capricious and unforgiving divine anger that has shaped human behavior for millennia. I tried closing paragraph after closing paragraph, but to no avail. Then, in a moment of inspiration, my editor suggested that I use an analogy with a supertanker, just as I had in the first chapter when I described such a huge vessel brushing aside a Bay of Biscay gale. Eureka! The analogy closed off *The Long Summer* beautifully, so well in fact that quite a few reviewers praised it.

It was only in the tenth draft that I got the chapter right and both the editor and I were satisfied. This brings us to our seventh rule of successful archaeology writing: revision is the essence of good writing, something often ignored and rarely explored in print.

I know a historian who claims with pride that when working on a book he writes a paragraph a day, which he considers publishable prose. When the book is finished, he reads it through once, then sends it to the publisher. Interestingly, every time we meet he complains of the demands of editors and quirks of copy editors. When he showed me a few pages of edited manuscript, it was clear that they were correcting grammatical errors, inconsistencies, and organizational problems he should have tackled in a revised draft. He gets away with this because he's an eminent scholar and his books sell well. We all have our ways of working, but I know I could never write his way. For most people, the crux of book writing is constant revision, for it is only then, when you stand back from the nitty-gritty of the first draft, that you can see the forest for the trees. Most of my books go through at least six to eight drafts, and the editors still find things to fix.

Revision, revision: this should be one of your writing mantras from day one. Here, for the record, are mine:

FAGAN'S WRITING MANTRAS

- Passion, passion.

- Always tell a story.

- Research with great care.

- Make writing a habit.

- Revise, revise . . . for accuracy and style.

- Eliminate, eliminate . . . irrelevant clutter.

- Meet your deadlines.

- Cherish your editors.

- Listen to criticism and act on it.

- Develop your own way of writing.

- Above all, write, write, write.

Revision Strategies

Harry Wolcott encapsulates the process of revision beautifully: "Some of the best advice I've ever found for writers happened to be included with the directions for assembling a new wheelbarrow: Make sure all parts are properly in place before tightening" (2001: 109). You must now ensure that all the parts are in place and articulating correctly. Are your arguments complete? Do you have all the data in place, the correct examples to bolster your narrative? Have you shortchanged one topic at the expense of others? Does everything come together in the way envisaged in your original passionate narrative and proposal? Sustained editing and revision is the only way of ensuring that the wheelbarrow, in this case your book, comes together as a seamless whole.

The revision strategy advocated in this chapter, and used to fine-tune this book, is only one of many. It works for me, but may not be appropriate for you. The process can be traumatic—you come across long, unnecessarily complex sentences, convoluted paragraphs, pithy phrases, and undue use of passive tenses that once seemed wonderful.

Some writers make a distinction between revising content and editing for style, with content coming first. This gives a mistaken impression of a two-part process, when in fact the two go together.

Here are a few useful revision strategies:

- Ask colleagues to read and edit the manuscript, a service you can also give them. This kind of editing is especially valuable in ensuring that all the parts fit together. If there are holes in your arguments, they'll find them.

- Edit successive drafts in small batches, so that you don't reach a point of diminishing return. Allow several days between each revision so that you come to it with a fresh mind.

- If deadlines press on you, consider editing the book from back to front, or reading the first draft aloud in an unfamiliar setting.

- First, line-edit word by word, then read the book quickly to gain an overall impression of it.

- A useful trick: change the arrangement of margins or paragraphs on a page or even the font to gain a different impression of sentences or paragraphs that are firmly entrenched in your mind.

- Try purely mechanical tactics like making a goal of removing two words from each sentence, or editing to eliminate a widow (two or three words in a separate line at the end of the paragraph). This strategy can tighten a manuscript dramatically, if used judiciously.

- Make a systematic effort to eliminate passive tenses. Focus your revision on repetitive phrases and words like "very."

- Employ a freelance editor to work with you on revision. This costs money (typically several dollars a page), but is well worth it if you can afford it—if you can find a good editor who is expert at improving comprehension without tampering with the content of the book. Your editor may know of several freelancers who undertake such work regularly and are used to working with academic authors.

The approach I use and describe here has evolved over years and works well for me. It's up to you to devise your own. In the end, however, the basics will remain the same, whatever strategies you use to refine the first draft.

Tackling the First Draft

After the first draft is complete, start thinking of the book in its entirety, rather than of individual chapters. Plan for the first-draft revision as an integrated whole, leaving other projects on the side while you are working on it. In this way, you'll get a sense of the general sweep of the book, the development of the idea, the themes, and the narrative flow. Look at the manuscript as a whole for the first time. Use a hard copy, so you can feel the manuscript and make pencil marks all over it. You can turn to the computer later.

You'll probably be appalled by the draft. (The first version of this book was truly awful.) Parts of it will read well, but all too much will be repetitive, perhaps confusing, and the arguments convoluted. This is hardly surprising, since you've focused so far on setting a draft on paper so that you can grasp the whole elephant. Don't feel overwhelmed. Some of the toughest work is behind you. The most pleasurable moments of authorship lie ahead.

I begin by reading through the hard copy quickly, to get a general sense of the narrative and subject matter. Then I read each chapter again and make corrections while compiling an outline of the paragraphs on a yellow pad.

Once you've made your hard-copy corrections, turn to the computer and go through the chapter again, entering your changes and making even more. The first revision is a large-scale, overall process, designed to refine your first draft into a coherent book. Don't worry about spelling mistakes and minor inconsistencies until they hit you in the face: they will be taken care of later. Concentrate on the flow of the story and the themes, the overall tautness of the narrative.

The initial run-through will almost certainly involve massive rewriting of large parts of the manuscript. Paragraphs are in the wrong order; your argument loses steam because you have omitted a key

WHAT TO LOOK FOR WHEN REVISING A MANUSCRIPT

- Check the flow of the arguments and narrative.

- Ensure the paragraph order is correct.

- Eliminate large-scale repetitions.

- Double-check that the content belongs in the chapter and that you have covered the key points.

- Identify major grammatical and stylistic problems.

- Cull unnecessary words, overused phrases, passive tenses, and unnecessary quotes.

- Establish where illustrations might be appropriate.

point; an important site has received inadequate coverage—to mention only a few potential difficulties. However, this time the writing will come more easily, because you already have a substantial core of text in hand which can be retained. You're tightening things, filling gaps.

Once again, follow a sedulous routine, allocating time every day for your work. Revision should be just as much a habit as writing the first draft, but with one difference: you'll cover more manuscript in a day because revision goes faster than composition. Don't allocate a number of words a day, just forge ahead to complete what's comfortable for you. Any revision, however light, requires intense concentration, because you are alternately looking at the broad sweep of the book and at minute detail. Some of the revision is going to be very challenging indeed. If you find yourself frustrated by a particularly difficult passage, leave it overnight and tackle it first thing in the morning when your mind's fresh.

This simple trick works like a charm. For example, I had great difficulty launching this chapter. At first I put the one-paragraph-a-day historian up-front, but it just didn't work. The next day, I wrote a paragraph about the achievement of completing the first draft. That didn't work either. I set it aside. The following morning, I tried *The Long Summer* paragraph and everything fell into place. A fresh mind solved the problem.

Another useful tip: each morning before you continue revising, quickly read through the material you worked on the day before. Don't correct anything or have second thoughts, unless there is something glaringly wrong. This will ensure continuity as you forge ahead.

Once this first run-through is complete, you should have your story in order, your arguments well marshaled and consistent, and the coverage complete. In other words, you have a pretty taut narrative in hand.

Once again, let the manuscript suffer from benign neglect for at least a week. Then you'll approach the all-important second edit with a fresh mind.

The Second Revision

The first revision is when the manuscript begins to become a book. The second one gives you a first sense of the final draft. Up to this point your focus has been on the ideas, the arguments, and the data. Now it's time to polish the text, once again revising chapter by chapter. Read slowly and meticulously, word for word, sentence by sentence, correcting every stylistic error, misspelling, or other minor sin you see. *The Chicago Manual of Style* is an invaluable assistant. Most publishers use it as a guide to rules for punctuation, spelling, and the like. It will save you a lot of trouble later on.

As you undertake the second pass, once again check the flow of the narrative and arguments, but pay careful attention to some important basics we have left aside so far.

Length

Your contract will have specified the estimated length of the book sought by the publisher, which is set in part by pricing considerations. It's your responsibility to keep to the agreed number of words, usually between 75,000 and 90,000, although some books can be considerably longer, especially textbooks. Perhaps you are writing a book in a series with an identical specification for each volume, perhaps as little as 30,000 to 45,000 words. The pricing of such volumes is carefully set upfront and there's little room for extra words. The word-count feature of your word-processing program will give you the figures. With printed pages, a ratio of four manuscript to three printed pages suffices for books without many illustrations. For the latter, the ratio is nearer 3:2.

Whatever the length, be careful to deliver to specification; otherwise you'll find yourself cutting at the copyedit stage, or the publisher will simply throw the manuscript back at you with a request for large cuts, often at the last minute. Slippage of a few thousand words with larger books is inevitable and accepted, but you must exercise discipline over your verbosity.

The best way to handle length issues is to aim at chapters of more or less standard length, unless a specific topic requires longer treatment. For instance, this book aims at 5,000 to 5,500 words per chapter. With longer books, I usually try to come in with chapter lengths of 6,000 words or so in the first draft, but invariably some are longer than others. By the time I reach the end of the second revision, the book is at more or less final length, although I tend to cut even more in the third run-through.

Don't fall into the trap of saying that your subject matter cannot possibly be covered in X number of words. Rest assured that it can be, provided you practice editorial discipline. I've learned a great deal about cutting from my New York editors, who are maestros of the editorial pen. They cut paragraphs that I could have sworn worked well, often because I'm inadvertently repeating myself. I also tend to be verbose and to use too many adjectives, which he seizes on with delight. (For more on the writer-editor relationship, see Chapter 5.)

Pacing

In Chapters 4 and 6, I talked about the importance of pacing, which gives critical life to a narrative. By varying the pace, you engage the readers with your story and keep their interest. The second-stage revision is where you should pay careful attention to pacing, looking for places where the manuscript seems flat and needs a personal experience, an example, even a short tangent to make things come alive. Pacing is something I think about right up to the final draft: it can make or break a story.

As You Read, Train Your Mind to Look for:

- Paragraphs and sentences that say the same thing, often in the same words, separated by several pages. You'd be amazed how often this happens, usually because you have a point to emphasize running through your head.

- Excessive use of the same phrase or word. For a while, I constantly referred to "a mosaic of" whatever I was discussing. Other phrases I now avoid: "Actually," "further afield," "cultural affinities," and "everything points to."

- Use of cliché sentences like "this leads us to believe that," and other such ghastly expressions. We all know what they are, for they haunt innumerable papers from graduate seminars. Many writers cling to them in later life.

- Excessive use of the passive tense; active tenses make for better narrative.

- Using the same word again and again on the same page. Yesterday, I caught myself using the word "routine" five times on one manuscript page.

- Excessive use of quotes, or too-long quotations.

- Grammatical errors, active and passive tenses, omitted words, incomplete sentences, punctuation, and, of course, typos. Use your spell checker with each draft, starting with this one. Then check in person. For instance, I spelled "diary" as "dairy." The spell checker passed it. A reviewer spotted the mistake.

Inconsistencies and Repetitions

Spotting inconsistencies and repetitions is an art at which copy editors, usually not authors, excel. You'll keep on finding them right up to the copyedit stage and wonder why you haven't seen them before. It's almost invariably because you're too close to the manuscript, whereas outsiders see things you don't. You need to develop a mind-set that constantly questions your narrative.

Illustrations

You should now finalize the illustrations and insert what are known as the "callouts" into the manuscript. Every publisher has its own house rules. A common way of calling out is as follows:

* * * Figure 5.1 goes here * * *

At this stage, too, draft the picture captions and place them at the end of the chapter.

References and Readings

You'll recall that I urged you to make notes for the references at first-draft stage. It's now time to put these into final form, knowing that they may be shifted around later on. Check with your editor as to the format the publishing house uses, which is normally either footnotes or the author-date style (e.g., Smith 1884). For general works, I prefer footnotes, which are less disruptive of the narrative. If you're asked to write an annotated bibliography, now's the time to compile it.

When you've completed the second revision, try reading the manuscript aloud, either in solitude, to a friend, or even to the cat. If there are clumsy arguments and poor sentence construction, your voice will find them.

As you drink a glass of sherry with an egg beaten up in it to revive your vocal cords (a recipe favored by P. G. Wodehouse's clergymen), set the manuscript aside for at least a week, and then . . .

Get Others to Read It

This is when you should seek external help. Ask several colleagues, at least one of them a scholar with related interests, to read the manuscript. Ask for frank comments, both general impressions and minor details. At the same time, see if you can find a non-archaeologist to read the book for you. Find a specific kind of reader, someone who is a ruthless critic and nitpicker, your worst nightmare as a potential critic. Such readers will soon tell you if they cannot understand something. If you can find someone who is a professional writer, all the better. I'm fortunate in that I have a writer friend who literally coaches me through manuscripts, a priceless relationship from which I learn every day. I hope you can find someone similarly helpful.

Ask your readers to scribble on the manuscript unmercifully and then discuss it with them over lunch. Then take all the comments and act on them. This is criticism that really counts, for it comes from people who know you well. Of course you'll reject some of their suggestions, but, for the most part, they'll have reactions that are an invaluable barometer of how your book will fare in the wider academic arena and in the world as a whole. If their comments are negative, so much the better in the long run. If you can look at them dispassionately, sift out the inevitable biases of the readers, and act on their suggestions, you'll have an immeasurably better manuscript at final-draft stage. There are, of course, writers with hefty egos who bristle at any criticism and brush aside critical comments as irrelevant. In fact, direct criticism will usually be less harsh than it sometimes should be, for fear of offense. Leave your ego at the door and pay careful attention to what your readers say—and to what peer reviewers contribute if such review is part of the publisher's editorial process.

The Final Draft

You'll probably go through at least four drafts before you feel that you have achieved the final one. One of them will incorporate the outside comments and involve a meticulous check for stylistic errors and typos. At this point, too, you should cross-check your references and illustration callouts. Make sure that the manuscript conforms to the publisher's house rules, which they should send you on request.

The last draft will be the final polish of the manuscript. Now read the book as if you were a reader, checking the broad sweep of the manuscript while casting a critical eye at the narrative and the style.

A Word on Prefaces

So far, we've said nothing about the preface, which is the single most important part of the entire manuscript from the marketing perspective. It is in these few pages that you must communicate the themes and argument of your book in such a way that busy readers will get an immediate sense as to what your book is about. A preface should be a road map to the book. Prefaces are also an important tool for busy reviewers and can make all the difference as to whether a book receives the full review treatment or is ignored.

Leave writing the preface to the very end, preferably to that moment when you are fresh off the final read-through of the manuscript and are full of enthusiasm, with a nice grasp of the themes and issues. Keep it short and to the point.

Preface writing is an art, one not easily mastered. Invariably, my editor rewrites mine completely, which is hardly surprising, since he has an outsider's perspective on the book and also a better sense of what people look for in prefaces. In the case of *The Long Summer*, which discussed long-term climatic and cultural change, the thorny issue of global warming was at center stage. I wrote briefly about how I was introduced to Ice Age climate change by an old-fashioned Cambridge University professor, and then wrote about the revolution in climatology and environmental determinism:

> You certainly cannot argue that climate drove history in a direct and causative way to the point of forcing major innovations or toppling entire civilizations. Nor, however, can one contend as many scholars once did that climate change is something that can be ignored. The dynamics of subsistence agriculture compel our attention. Ever since the beginnings of farming some 12,000 years ago, people have lived at the mercy of cycles of cooler and wetter, warmer and drier climate.

Their survival depended on crop yields and on having enough seed to plant for the next year. . . . Climate is, and always has been, a powerful catalyst in human history, a pebble cast in a pond whose ripples triggered all manner of economic, political and social changes. (Fagan 2004b:xiv)

Then I developed a central theme of the book—vulnerability to climate change—and ended the preface by saying:

Looked at in this light, the present problem of global warming is neither proof of late capitalism's intent to commit industrial-strength sins against Mother Earth nor a hallucination imposed on the world by anti-business activists. It is simply a reflection of our scale of vulnerability, the scale on which we must now think and act. The times require us to learn the vagaries of the global climate, to study its moods, and to keep our skies relatively clear of excessive greenhouse gasses with the same diligence, and for the same reasons, that Mesopotamian farmers five millennia ago had to learn the moods of the Euphrates and keep their irrigation canals reasonably free of silt. . . . Sooner or later, they got unlucky and were forced to adapt yet again. This book is the story of these adaptations, one built upon another, in a spiral of climate change and human response that continues today. (Fagan 2004b:xv–xvi)

The Long Summer's preface laid out the themes of a book that placed more than ten millennia of human adaptation in the context of modern global warming. An essay of just over five pages did the job.

Submission

Before you send anything off, make backups and copies of everything and file them safely away, and then pack up the book.

In your cover letter, specifically request acknowledgment that the editor has received the manuscript. I always send manuscripts by FedEx, UPS, or some other courier service, rather than by US mail. Most publishers routinely use these services, for the reliability is superb. The day you dispatch the package, e-mail your editor and tell him or her when to expect it.

WHAT YOUR MANUSCRIPT PACKAGE SHOULD INCLUDE

■ A cover letter to the editor, listing the contents of the package.

■ A hard copy of the manuscript, complete with references and illustration callouts, the picture legends being at the end of each chapter, along with any sidebars and boxes. Please make sure that this is pristine, with no handwritten manuscript corrections. The publisher's production department will love you!

■ A hard copy of the grayscale images and line drawings, and color pictures if you are allowed them.

■ CDs of the manuscript and illustrations, the latter being in high-resolution format as specified by the publisher. Most contracts specify that the author is responsible for drawings at production standard.

■ A master list of the picture captions, with credits and also an indication of the desired size for each illustration: ¼, ½, full-page, etc. This gives production staff a sense of the importance of the drawing or photograph.

■ A permissions file of any copyrighted material, usually pictures, with evidence that permission fees have been paid if this is the author's responsibility.

■ A brief author biography (no more than two paragraphs) and picture. This is for the back cover or dust jacket.

And Now What Happens?

Usually silence—it takes time for your editor to read through the manuscript and to formulate comments. All editors handle several books at once, and you are just one in the queue.

If you're working with a university press, the editor may send your book out for review while he or she also works on the manuscript. Then weeks or even months later, you'll receive an editorial letter accompanied by the anonymous reviews from outside academics. The editor will amplify points raised by the reviewers and draw your attention to parts of the book that need the most attention, but will probably not line-edit, a task left to copy editors. You are on your own and will have to complete your rewriting and editing by yourself. Most editors will call you to discuss the manuscript. Be prepared to take detailed notes, for verbal comments are often more valuable than written ones, especially if you are trying to identify the biases—even, dare I say it, sometimes the agendas—of reviewers.

With general trade houses, you will receive a detailed editorial reaction, which will usually take the form of a letter itemizing the major points of concern. This may be accompanied by a line-edit of the manuscript, although this is becoming rarer in this day and age of promiscuous book writing and overworked editors. If you are lucky enough to have an old-fashioned editor who really believes in line-editing and working with the author, give thanks, for they are priceless assets. I've been fortunate to work with my latest editor on three books, each of which he line-edited with a perception that at times took my breath away. He has a wonderful sense of a book, something that only an outsider can see. On several occasions, I have been in despair over a chapter, only to have him pull it together with a judicious sentence or timely paragraph that proves to be the missing link in the narrative chain. Sometimes, these line-edits can be brutal, but they improve the manuscript immeasurably.

The Final Manuscript

With editor's (and perhaps peer reviewers') comments in hand, you're ready to tackle the last revision. If the comments are numerous, or if you have a full line-edit to work through, the task will seem overwhelming, so break the job down into manageable segments.

Tackle the minor nitpicks first—factual errors, typos, and minor stylistic corrections. Then they're out of the way. This should be a straightforward task that proceeds fairly rapidly. Make free use of global search-and-replace features if you have spelled site names wrong or made some other similar error. Once these minor corrections are made, you should be in the mood to start on major surgery.

Major changes can range from a request for a complete rewrite of one or several chapters, even of the entire book, to just reworking a subsection or a specific passage. One can break them down into two broad categories—internal modifications in chapters and complete rewrites.

As the second order of business, I usually work on the internal changes. Many of them may seem like formidable undertakings, but in practice they often require little more than rewriting a couple of paragraphs, adding a subtle nuance to a ten-line discussion, or perhaps giving more space to an alternative theory that you have overlooked. A reviewer may suggest some references of which you were unaware. Again, these should not prove insurmountable tasks and are often an invaluable preparation for the major rewrites. In many cases, you can identify the mind-set of a reviewer or editor from the consistency of his or her comments. On occasion, too, you may have to mediate between the competing views of several reviewers. I once had six peer reviews of a book where all the reviewers disagreed with one another— and with me! Talk about navigating perilous academic minefields. Fortunately, my editor helped me through the morass in a series of long telephone conversations and faxes.

By the time you confront the major rewrites, your mind should be keenly focused on the manuscript and the revision blessed with a comfortable momentum. You've tamed a seemingly huge beast and reduced it to reasonable proportions. Almost invariably, the rewrite request will focus on individual chapters. Only once have I been asked for a complete rewrite on the grounds that the manuscript "did not include enough hard science." On that occasion, I fought back and won, but it was a hollow victory, for the book didn't sell well anyhow.

If you are asked for a complete rewrite, think carefully about the reasons for it. Remember that your editor is a mediator between you, the specialist, and your general audience. He or she is the advocate for the reader. Ask yourself, as he or she does: what does the reader expect to get out of the book? This is a different question from the corollary: what story do I want to tell? In most cases, the editor is probably correct in his or her perceptions, or there is some basic misunderstanding (as there was in the case of my rewrite). Please don't assume that you know better than the editor. You probably don't. Talk to him or her before starting, or, if you possibly can, meet face-to-face to talk the revision through.

Chapter revisions are more straightforward, for you follow the recommendations of the editor. With rewrites, I recommend the 1,000-word-a-day routine, which again cuts the task up into smaller portions. For example, a chapter in the final manuscript of *Fish on Friday* raised serious editorial concerns, specifically about the date of the first discovery of the Newfoundland cod fisheries. The only solution was a complete rewrite and the collapsing together of two chapters, a task that occupied a tense six days and some frantic reading of obscure sources. All was well in the end. The editor sent back the new version with only minor corrections.

All revisions of this nature are compromises between author and publisher. You are never going to agree with everything that the other parties suggest, nor should you. A good, accurate manuscript lies somewhere between the two extremes of your final draft and the version of the book envisaged by the editor. The art of being a good author requires that you dispassionately attempt to make your manuscript truly publishable and worthy of your talents. This is not an easy task by any standards, but it's a deeply satisfying one when you receive an e-mail or phone call that says, "Brian, *Fish* has been released to production today." Finally, all the hard work seems worth it.

You cannot relax yet, for you still have to navigate the shoals of production and the challenges of helping to market your book in an overcrowded archaeological marketplace, issues discussed in the next chapter.

PRODUCTION AND BEYOND

Rule 8: Don't walk away from your book when you finish writing it.

YOUR BOOK IS RELEASED for production and you heave a giant sigh of relief. The battle is o'er, the victory won—or is it? You still have a great deal of work ahead of you as your manuscript advances through production. Even when you finally have the printed book in your hands, the issue of marketing arises. This chapter discusses the production process and also some of the steps you can take to help market your book. The focus here is on trade books, but the process closely resembles that for academic books and for textbooks, with the difference that the latter are more heavily illustrated and more complex. We discuss some of the challenges of textbook production in Chapter 9.

Production and Production Editors

Book production has become shorter and more streamlined with the advent of computers. What took nine months to a year or more can now be completed accurately and efficiently within six months or even less, depending on the publishing house. Even so, your manuscript spends much of this time waiting in line for attention. Large trade and textbook publishers have refined production into an assembly-line process that turns out books like sausages, many of them sharing similar design templates. Many of the books that come off this kind of conveyor belt look nice and give an impression of high quality. Even small houses now produce books with as much standardization as possible. Like their larger compatriots, they are sensitive to retail price points in the marketplace and to inexorably rising costs.

Until now, you'll have dealt with the editor who signed your book. Although he or she will still be involved in the project, the primary responsibility now falls on your production editor, who does nothing but shepherd books through production. Many production departments are not even in the same building as the editorial department. For example, the subsidiaries of Perseus Books, one of my trade publishers, have editorial offices on the East Coast. But all production is handled in Boulder, Colorado. In these days of air freight, e-mail, and electronic manuscripts, the cost savings are substantial. Many publishers have contracted production operations offshore. I regularly have manuscripts designed and laid out in India.

At an early stage in the production process, you'll receive an e-mail, letter, or phone call from your production editor identifying himself or herself as the person in charge of your book as it goes through the mill. This communication will give you some details of the process and lay out the approximate production schedule. You will probably learn the dates when you'll expect to receive the copyedit, your first reunion with your manuscript after formal submission.

Production editors are the anonymous heroes of publishing and some of the most important people in your writing life. I have one textbook production editor who has worked on nine manuscripts for me and counting. We can read each other's thoughts on the phone, but we have never met. With her calm attention to detail, she makes my books immeasurably better. With production editors, think teamwork and cooperation. They thrive on efficiency and attention to detail.

Production editors appreciate personal contact and a caring author at the other end. Make a point of calling directly after you receive an initial e-mail or letter from them. Tell them you're calling to say hello, to ask if they have any immediate questions, and to reassure them that you'll deliver everything they ask for on deadline. I always make a point of stressing that I hope they will always tell me if they are not satisfied with my responses, that I will never take such criticism personally. Remember that you are dealing with a human being who takes enormous pride in his or her work and often gets little credit for it. And when the advance copy arrives, be sure to call and say how much you like the final product. A confirming e-mail asking him or her to extend your thanks to everyone involved in the book is a small gesture, but it means more to the production team than you can imagine. They labor in quiet, hardworking anonymity and often receive only criticism, even abuse. Please—be one of the nice authors.

As your book advances through production, you'll usually have two contact points with your manuscript—the copyedit stage and the proofs.

Copyedit

Your production editor will probably not contact you until the due date of the copyedit is established in-house. After it arrives and has been checked, the copyedited manuscript will be sent out to you with a request that you review and return it by a deadline of between ten days and three weeks. The editor will specify a specific return date. Make sure that you have the manuscript back in his or her hands by the deadline, lest your production schedule be thrown off. Large publishers work closely with their printers, who allocate them tight manufacturing slots. Everything functions on economies of scale.

Copy editors are a unique breed, almost all of them specialist freelancers who do nothing but dissect manuscripts line by line, page by page. I've found that they have a mind-set for detail, an eerie ability to spot inconsistencies hundreds of pages apart, and a maddening tendency to make you feel careless, your writing clumsy. Good copy editors are worth their weight in gold. Their queries may drive you crazy, but they know what they are talking about.

You'll receive your copyedited manuscript festooned with corrections, editorial rewrites, changes to conform to house rules, and queries. Many publishers now send you an electronic copyedit, where the editor makes corrections on-screen, directly into your manuscript file, identifying the changes with lines and symbols like <aq> ("author query," indicating a question from the copy editor to the author, who needs to respond) in the margin. Other houses, especially textbook publishers, still send you a hard copy of the manuscript with the editor's changes in colored pencil and numerous yellow stickies that ask questions. These examples come from one of my recent copyedits:

> **Au:** Is it Basketmaker or Basket Maker? Please check msp 33, 122, 124 and correct inconsistency.
>
> **Au:** Sentence correct as amended? Please check for correct meaning.

When you receive the copyedit, take a deep breath and be prepared to go through the manuscript line by line. Set up a routine for going through the edit, so that you complete it well ahead of time, working on, say, one or two chapters a day. There is no easy way to cope with a copyedit. The detail is mind-numbing and the persistent queries will get to you, which is why you should ration your daily dose.

WHAT COPY EDITORS DO

- Check the manuscript to see that it conforms to publishing house rules of punctuation, spelling, etc.

- Make changes where appropriate to improve grammar, punctuation, style, and comprehension, but not rewrite.

- Check for inconsistencies, repeats, and correct order of paragraphs.

- Ensure that all illustration callouts and cross-references are correct and that the legends and illustrations are in place.

- Check all bibliographic references, glossary definitions, etc., for consistency, but not accuracy.

Every author I know has a different way of approaching the work. I go through each chapter dealing with the minor queries, where I often need do little more than write "OK" on a sticky or in the margins. In other cases, I need to approve an edited sentence or word order, allow a deletion or the moving of a sentence or paragraph. As I deal with the minor queries, I simply flag the major ones that require additional research to answer (for instance, what was the date of this event?) or rewriting of a page or more, and do them afterward. I can then work through the lengthier queries without distraction.

This is the last chance you have to make significant changes to the manuscript before it is typeset and paginated. But this does not mean that you have an excuse to rewrite the book yet again. As you read through the copyedit, check your facts one last time, if necessary add a few sentences about essential new discoveries or theories since you completed the final draft, and that is that. Your changes should be limited to short passages; otherwise you'll affect production costs at a point when the budget is already set. Should you be in a position where substantive changes are needed involving a paragraph or two, or several pages, contact your sponsoring editor for approval, not the production editor. You should go into the copyedit with the firm notion that what you have written is final.

Stories abound of authors throwing temper tantrums over their copyedited manuscripts, on the grounds that the editor has murdered their meticulously calibrated prose. There are those who fight the copy editors page after page, often over trivial questions of style and punctuation. In the wider scheme of things, such battles are rarely worth fighting, for the stakes are low and house rules often apply. Is it really worth quarreling over southern Africa or Southern Africa? People do, and it's just dumb. Remember that most copy editors use a standard reference guide like *The Chicago Manual of Style*—they don't make up the rules. It's much better to raise questions when there is an important misunderstanding or a consistent problem. A question like this often arises when a copy editor has simply misunderstood you. He or she will usually be happy to accommodate your concerns. Better to win the important battles than to dally in skirmishes. And if the sponsoring editor agrees with the copy editor, then surrender gracefully.

Almost invariably, I've found that copy editors are competent people who really care about books. Only once have I had a serious problem—with an editor who loaded my style with consistently passive tenses. It transpired that she was used to editing science books, not narrative. We sorted the problem out with a couple of phone calls and all was well.

Above all, be pleasant and always polite—and make a point of asking your production editor to pass on your thanks for a job well done. Copy editors deserve an author's gratitude.

Illustrations

At this point we should go on a short tangent and talk about illustrations, which we have hitherto left aside. This is an appropriate point to do so, for it is at the post-copyedit stage that line drawings and photographs come to the fore.

Archaeology is a visual discipline, which means that books on the subject are more heavily illustrated than others. In recent years, trade publishers in particular have cut back on the number of photographs in their books on grounds of cost, so you have to be creative about the pictures you choose. But remember the old adage that a picture is worth a thousand words.

Line Drawings

Archaeology is about obscure places, so good maps are essential. Remember that even well-informed readers may not know where Mesa Verde or Teotihuacán is located, let alone Pergamon or Paracas. Distribution maps are important when discussing changing societies, as are environmental drawings that show positions of ice sheets, low sea levels, and other major features of the ancient world. Clear, well-designed maps are the most important illustrations in your book.

Diagrams should be used sparingly and only to make a point in your narrative or to amplify it in a meaningful way. Numeric tables are usually meaningless to the general reader, but a diagram showing the walking distance between villages on an island, for example, is invaluable and can save a lot of words.

All too many archaeological books are laden with sterile artifact drawings that are of little interest to anyone but a specialist. You can safely omit most artifact drawings except for critically important or spectacular ones. A Clovis point or a drawing of a Magdalenian engraving would fall into this category. Use line drawings to amplify your story, not for aesthetic reasons.

Most publishers expect you to submit graphics and maps that are ready for production. In these days of desktop publishing, you can do this yourself or hire a graphic designer to produce them. If you are using numbers of maps and diagrams, you may be best off hiring a professional to ensure consistency. Proofread both your roughs and final versions carefully; your artist will not be familiar with cultural names and obscure locations, and you, not the copy editor, are responsible for their accuracy. TIFF file format is usually preferred, but it's important to check the publisher's guidelines for the correct one to use. Line art should be scanned at a minimum of 1200 dpi. Most publishers prefer files created in Adobe Illustrator or Photoshop.

Indicate on your legend master sheet what size you would like them reproduced—quarter page, half page, and so on. This gives the production people a sense of the importance of the illustration to the narrative. Always send a printout of each image as a reference copy, as this makes the production process easier for someone unfamiliar with the manuscript. Burn everything on a CD-ROM.

If you want an example of superb line drawings, take a look at Egyptologist Barry Kemp's *Ancient Egypt: The Anatomy of a Civilization* (2006). Kemp uses three-dimensional renderings of such important sites as the Step Pyramid of Saqqara to show the relationships among the different ceremonial structures and spaces that served not only as a royal mortuary, but as a setting for important royal ceremonials. Kemp's drawings complement the text brilliantly.

Photographs

Unless you are writing a coffee-table book (a genre unto itself) or some form of more lavish volume, such as many of the beautifully illustrated books produced by Thames & Hudson, the world's leading archaeological publishers, you're almost certainly working with halftones (black-and-white photographs). Academic monographs and syntheses tend to be heavily illustrated with photographs of excavations, structures, artifacts, and the like which are too technical or irrelevant to more general works. Photographs are usually rationed in trade books, so you will have to take care in choosing them. Generally speaking, they fall into these general categories:

- **Location photographs** that give the reader a general sense of the environments and settings in which your story unfolds. Examples: a shot of a New York City block where important excavations have taken place, or Hadrian's Wall snaking over ridges in northern England. Make sure the picture is evocative and takes the reader into the place.

- **Excavation and fieldwork shots.** If you're talking about such subjects, you need a couple of shots that show a survey or dig in progress. Keep these to a decent minimum. Images of people excavating houses, burials, or whatever are now almost cliché unless there's a specific tale behind the work—a bulldozer approaching, or some such thing. One of the most effective shots of an excavation I've ever seen is Adriel Heisey's brilliant aerial photograph of an excavation of a Hohokam village in the center median of Interstate 10 near Tucson, Arizona. Using an ultralight aircraft, Heisey took an overhead shot of the block excavation, showing houses and features in the central median. A few meters away, a large truck passes by at 55 mph. He has captured the essence of CRM.

- **The archaeological record.** Again, keep these images to a minimum if you're writing about shell middens, caves, or other unspectacular sites. Photographs of the Cliff Palace at Mesa Verde or Cahokia are another matter, but, again, don't overdo it. The reader needs a sense of the record, no more.

- **Artifacts.** Keep artifact images to a minimum. Spectacular objects are often hoary old favorites, such as the Moche portrait heads from Peru, Tutankhamun's throne, or the perfectly preserved La Tène horned helmet from the River Thames in London. Then there are artifacts that tell a story, such as superb Maya vases and the complex ideologies unrolled photographically off Moche pots. Here, you can use a caption to tell a secondary story to your narrative. Whenever you illustrate an artifact, be sure to explain its importance.

■ **Technical shots.** Edge wear on stone tools, ethnoarchaeology, details of architecture—the limit is your imagination. Again, keep the photographs to a minimum and use them only when you can add a judicious caption to amplify something in the narrative. Think of such captions as mini-tangents.

Unless you've taken the photographs yourself, you'll have to get permission to reproduce them from the person or organization that owns the rights. While most photographic agencies work efficiently online, allowing you to purchase an image in seconds, many individuals and organizations are much slower. You will probably be able to deal with them by e-mail. Allow plenty of time for the process, which can take weeks, even months. Your publisher will have a standard permission request form—usually in the "rights and permissions" section of their web page—which spells out what you are requesting. There are all kinds of rights, each with different costs—everything from world rights, all languages, to North America only. Ask your editor for advice on the rights you should seek.

A typical permissions letter is addressed to the rights and permissions department of a publisher, or to the photographic department of a museum or university, or to an individual. (Check their web sites for the correct person to address or the form to use.) The letter gives the title and author of the book, the proposed publication date, publisher, anticipated print run, retail price, and specifies the rights requested as well as the size of reproduction anticipated, from one-eighth of a page and up.

In their reply, the organization will specify the cost of providing a print or scan and the amount of the reproduction fee. Normally, they won't sign off on the permission until the fee is paid. Photographic fees are rising rapidly, since organizations like the British Museum have realized that they offer a useful revenue stream. They sometimes run as high as $250 or more, depending on the market for your book, the image, and the institution. You can keep permission fees low by being creative and working with colleagues, but poor-quality images reflect adversely on your book. Who pays permission fees is a matter between you and your publisher. Some houses acquire the pictures and pay for everything, but this is rare. Most expect the author to pay all, or at least part, of the fees. Sometimes your contract with the publisher will specify an allowance for permissions, beyond which you pay.

The publisher will expect a file of signed copyright forms submitted with your manuscript, so they have a record that you have authority to reproduce the images.

Consult publishers' guidelines for their photographic requirements. Most houses now ask for scanned images, 5 × 7-inch glossy photographs, or slides. Scanned images are probably best, at a resolution of 400 dpi or above. It's advisable to send a test file for the publisher to check before you burn everything on a CD-ROM, and accompany it with a printout of each image for reference.

With all art, be sure to key the drawing or picture to the legends and callouts; otherwise chaos will result.

The Cover

Do not expect to have any input into the cover design or any image that appears thereon, although most publishers will welcome suggestions for cover pictures. The cover is usually designed way ahead of time, often before the book goes into production. This is because the publisher needs it for brochure design and advance sales work, activities that begin earlier than production of the book itself. If you have a favorite photo, or a cover suggestion, feel free to offer it, but don't be surprised if the publisher chooses something else.

Proofs

The last time you'll see your book before it's published is when you receive proofs. In the past, you had two runs at the proofs, at galley stage before pagination, and then as page proofs. This gave you a double-check on typos and other errors. Thanks to computers and desk-top publishing software, you now receive only typeset pages. As with the copyedit, you'll have only limited time to correct them, which you should do with sedulous care. Check for the less obvious things: the correct placement of illustrations and legends, and correct orientation of pictures (especially those of artifacts). If a picture seems unaccept-ably dark or light, don't worry, as production will correct that in-house. But if something looks particularly bad, it's worth mentioning it.

As the publisher will emphasize, do not make any editorial changes. You will be billed for these by the line. At this point your book is locked, except for typos and other production errors.

Many houses hire a professional proofreader to read the pages in parallel, which is nice insurance, as he or she is bound to find things that you miss (and vice versa).

The front matter and back-end pages and index will probably, but not invariably, come to you separately, after you have returned the main body of the proofs.

Index

Your contract will probably call for the author to prepare the index. Even in these days of electronic indexing, this is a time-consuming, tiresome process. If you do it yourself, consult an indexing guide (see "Resources for Writers" in the back of this book) and acquire the appropriate software. Most publishers will allow you to pay for an indexer to make yours, and I strongly recommend doing so. Such spe-cialists generally do a better job, as they have the experience and skills that are required. It's often a false economy to do this yourself. You will, of course, have an opportunity to check their work.

And then, finally . . .

Publication

Publication has two stages from your point of view. The first comes on that magical day when an advance copy of the book arrives and you finally have the finished product. A few weeks later, you'll receive the free copies called for under your contract. The second stage is the formal publication date, when the book has been distributed to bookstores, Amazon.com, and other outlets, a process that takes several weeks. This is when the publisher fulfills advance orders that have been solicited before publication. You have nothing to do except page through your new book and even read it. Inevitably, you'll spot a typo. Relax, there's nothing you can do about it. Be glad you're not in the position of a former colleague of mine, whose first book appeared with the author's name spelled wrong on the cover! Make sure that you keep a list of errors for the publisher to correct in possible reprints and new editions, such as a paperback version.

One thing remains: a quick phone call to both the editor and the production editor to thank them for all their hard work and for the end product. Surprisingly few authors extend this courtesy, which is deeply appreciated, especially by the anonymous, hardworking people who labor behind the scenes.

Marketing and Promotion

The Author Questionnaire

At some point during production, the publisher will send you an author questionnaire to fill out. This is a vitally important document, for its content determines a great deal of the marketing of your book. Fill it in as thoroughly as you can, to the point of overkill.

A typical author questionnaire asks for personal contact information, along with a summary of your book in 250 to 350 words (used to develop catalog and other copy) and other background information, such as incidents or experiences that unfolded during the research or details of the major themes of the book. You may be asked about the strengths and weaknesses of competing titles, if any, and for the names of people who might "blurb" the book on the cover and journals that could review it, and so on. The more complete the information you provide, the better marketing job the salespeople will do for you. You'll also have to provide an author photograph for the cover.

Now Your Book Is Out . . .

Once your book appears, the publisher will list it in the catalog, maybe solicit some mail-order sales through a special mailing, and post your title on the Web. If they exhibit at conventions, your book will appear on their stand as long as it's in print. You'll find your title on Amazon.com, Barnes and Noble.com, and other online outlets.

But the promotion budget for your book will likely be small, unless it is aimed at a wider readership. Even then, promotion is so expensive that the budget will probably be minimal. The big promotion monies go into mass-market volumes. Books by well-known authors like Jared Diamond and Dava Sobel come to mind, also the rare titles that are perceived to have bestseller potential. Your book will mainly sell on the basis of word of mouth, or perhaps from reviews in prominent outlets like the *New York Times Book Review*.

Reviews. There are so many books out there that it's getting harder and harder to obtain review exposure, even for important titles. Newspaper book-section space is shrinking as well, so count yourself lucky if you get reviewed in the *Los Angeles Times*, *Washington Post*, or some other major daily. *Time* and *Newsweek* review selected titles, especially those that are unusual or of current interest. Local newspapers often carry reviews, but, for the most part, they are short, at most a paragraph or two. A review in *Kirkus*, *Library Journal*, or *Publisher's Weekly* can make a significant difference, as librarians read them.

A great deal of reviewing now takes place on the Web, including Amazon.com, whose volunteer reviewers are often quirky, frequently biased, and, frankly, sometimes out to lunch.

One way or the other, you'll probably receive a few reviews, for which you should be thankful. If your book is published in England or other parts of Europe, your chances of a review are much higher, as such things are taken more seriously over there. Academic reviews generally appear months, even years, after publication and have little effect on sales.

You're naïve if you expect uniformly good reviews. There will be nitpickers, reviewers with agendas, and people who just plain disagree with you. My late father, in his day an eminent publisher, gave me the best advice the first time I received a stinker: roll with the punches, never respond unless specifically invited to do so, and move on. Even if asked to react, I would decline. Bad reviews are part and parcel of a writer's life. Remember that they are transitory phenomena, soon forgotten.

If your publisher pushes your book more aggressively, you may be faced with several additional activities:

Book tours. The publisher sends you on an East Coast, West Coast, or national tour, during which you appear on TV talk shows, on radio programs, and at book signings. Tours are grinding work and it's questionable how effective they are unless you are a big name. These days author tours are a vanishing breed, as they are very expensive. You're unlikely to be sent on one unless your book really takes off or has significant advance buzz. If you are selected for a tour, the publisher will arrange for a handler to escort you in each city, to make sure you get where you are supposed to be.

Book signings. Book signings are commonplace these days and involve you appearing at a bookstore, sometimes talking or reading from your book, and signing books. Occasionally, these are spectacularly successful, with as many as a hundred people there. Sometimes no one appears. It's Russian roulette and they are not worth traveling long distances for. Be sure, however, to do a signing in your home community as a courtesy to local business. Tell your publisher if you are traveling while your book is being marketed, to see if they want to set something up.

TV talk shows. A two- to five-minute interview as part of a news program or talk show is something you may encounter, especially at the local level. How effective they are is questionable. If you appear on *60 Minutes*, *The Colbert Report*, or *The Daily Show with Jon Stewart*, then you are really in business. Dream on. . . .

Radio and Web interviews. Radio is the best medium for promoting books, as you have a captive audience in their cars. Many talk shows like authors as guests and can have you on for as much as an hour, even for as long as three hours—in the middle of the night. (It's amazing how many of your friends listen to the radio at 2 A.M.!) If the interviewer is well prepared, the interview can be a positive, even enjoyable experience. Some are disasters, like the call-in show when a caller asked me if I was expecting the Second Coming of Christ in a fiery climate change, or when I was accused of being a racist because I said that Tutankhamun was not black! Public radio stations are especially effective for radio promotion, for the interviews tend to last longer, are much listened to, and the interviewers are well prepared.

Many radio shows will interview you by phone. The time differences may play havoc with your sleep patterns, as they often need you at exactly 4 A.M. your time. I have even done international interviews with simultaneous translation, which are fascinating experiences.

Web interviews are a relatively new phenomenon, but they are likely to be commonplace in the future.

Whatever medium you appear on, please be passionate, polite, and patient with sometimes idiotic questions. If you are irritated by the circus, keep in mind that these forums do sell books.

These remarks refer to trade books, not to texts, which are marketed entirely differently, through college bookstores. We enter the world of textbooks in Chapter 9.

TEXTBOOKS

Rule 9: Never write a textbook unless
you have the time to revise it.

S OONER OR LATER, a publisher will ask you to write a textbook. This happened to me only three weeks into my teaching career. I lamented to a visiting editor about the lack of good archaeology textbooks. The next thing I knew I was writing one on method and theory, an agonizing process that took five years. I must have done something right. *In the Beginning* (Fagan 2009) is still in print in a twelfth edition. Textbooks have been part of my archaeological life ever since.

Over the years, I've written a stable of textbooks with varying success. Each has a life of its own and stories that go with it. *Ancient Lives: An Introduction to Archaeology and Prehistory* (Fagan 2010a) is a case in point. The book began as a medium-sized method and theory text, written for HarperCollins as part of a concern that the major books, like *In the Beginning* and its competitors, were becoming too encyclopedic. Soon after the book appeared, HarperCollins sold its anthropology list to Prentice Hall. *Ancient Lives* did not do well. My new editor and I mulled over the future of the book. Should we kill it and focus on the other method and theory text? Or could we transform it into something else? We were having breakfast in a Denver hotel when a light went off in our collective heads. What about a combined, short method and theory and world prehistory text? I went away and fiddled with the idea. An outline came together beautifully and we went ahead. Today, *Ancient Lives*, now in its fourth edition, is a success with an established market niche.

There are intangible rewards in writing textbooks. You meet a broad cross section of archaeologists, many of them far from your own specialty. You learn a great deal about teaching in different institutions and about students. Above all, you develop a much broader grasp of archaeology than you had before. You find you can actually have intelligent conversations with specialists in all parts of the world. And, perhaps, one day you'll receive the ultimate reward, when a young colleague sidles up to you at a conference and confesses to having first met his or her chosen specialty in the pages of your text. With a bit of luck, the naïve freshman who is entranced by your introductory text today is tomorrow's specialist in medieval rabbit-keeping in France.

The college editors from the large publishing houses tour campuses, looking for potential authors. They're under constant pressure to sign new texts and identify professors to write that elusive, best-selling book that will dominate the marketplace. Sometimes it's hard to resist the siren call of an editor in full flow, especially when he or she dangles tantalizing advances and other perks in front of you. There's something seductive about becoming an authoritative voice for thousands of eager students. And there's always the (usually false) editor's lure of fat royalty checks. Can I, after all, drive a BMW instead of a Ford? If truth be told, few textbook authors make large sums. In these competitive, market-crowded days, they are lucky if their book survives a first edition. No one in their right mind writes a textbook because they want to make money. They write them because they perceive a need, or because they relish the challenge.

You need elemental courage to write a textbook. Textbooks rank low on the intellectual totem pole. The authorship of a text, however brilliant and timely, does not "count" in the narrowly defined world of academic publication. One hears that writing such books is "too easy," or an "inappropriate activity" for an academic researcher, the mark of a lightweight intellectual. What arrogant, self-serving nonsense! Textbook writing is among the hardest of all intellectual challenges. To write a successful textbook requires an ability to think and write clearly, not to mention a grasp of the broad issues of the subject matter beyond one's specialty. An aptitude for elegant classroom lecturing may help, but your real expertise must be in putting words to paper. As textbook editors soon learn, academics who have the gift of such writing are a rare breed, especially if they have academic visibility, a reputation as a basic researcher, and the other credentials that make them a force among their colleagues.

If you're determined to write a text, realize that any textbook project, even a short paperback, is going to involve a great deal of often heartbreaking, hard work, an ability to accept criticism, and, above all, a commitment to deliver the manuscript on time. The business of selling textbooks is quite unlike selling in bookstores or on the Web. There are two major seasons for textbook adoptions. Each falls about four to six months preceding the next school term, when professors turn in their textbook orders to the bookstore. New books must be available in the publisher's warehouse and in their sales force's hands at the beginning of these short and intense selling seasons, ready to ship to interested instructors. Thus, timely delivery—something often alien to academic authors—is of the essence.

How Textbooks Are Sold

There are none of the author tours, book signings, and TV appearances that are part and parcel of trade marketing. Selling textbooks is a highly structured, competitive business that works differently from trade marketing. While students purchase the books, they are not the decision makers; their instructors are. The magic word here is adoptions—persuading instructors or adoption committees to "adopt" your book, making it, as opposed to its competitors, required reading for the course.

The marketing process begins with your author questionnaire, where you should be careful to provide thoughtful, brief analyses of competing titles and stress the unique features of your book. Your responses form the basis for the relevant pages of the sales manual given to the publisher's field representatives. Your editor uses the same information, along with his or her own perceptions, to present the book to the assembled sales force at the annual or semiannual sales meetings, which take place at the beginning of the selling seasons. Sometimes you'll be asked to make a presentation at the sales meeting, but usually only if you have written a major introductory text with large sales potential.

In providing information to your publisher, it's crucial that you provide close comparisons to your competitors. What does your book do that others don't? What features does yours have that theirs lack? What can your field representative say to potential adopters in a minute or less—a brief sound bite—that highlights the unique selling points of your book? You need to know the competing books as well as your own to be able to make this pitch effectively.

Realize that your book is one of dozens of texts that the salespeople have to present during their campus visits. They will probably be visiting chemistry and literature instructors as well as archaeologists. Anything you can do to make yours stand out from the crowd, make it something that they think they can successfully sell, is useful.

As soon as your book appears, the publisher will send out classroom examination copies to every possible adopter of the text in the country in the hope of drawing attention to the book. Depending on the publication date, it may arrive before or after the sales reps move out into their territories and visit campus after campus. Good salespeople spend a great deal of time getting to know instructors in their territory, developing relationships in which they will be taken seriously. Editors travel, too, and are often a key factor in securing good adoptions. Textbook publishers also exhibit at major conventions like those of the American Anthropological Association and Society for American Archaeology. Spend some time at your publisher's booth, for you'll receive feedback and, at the same time, meet either existing users or potential adopters. You can be one of the publisher's most effective sales weapons by expressing your passion for what you have written to potential buyers.

Personal contact with publishers' reps is the most effective sales technique for textbooks, but the high cost of maintaining sales forces means that mail-order and Web marketing are assuming increasing importance. For smaller textbook publishers, or for textbooks designed for higher-level courses, direct mail, sample copies, telemarketing, convention displays, and Web announcements usually supplant the sales visits entirely.

From the author's perspective, however, a reputation for top-quality content, proper pedagogical concern, and a track record of successful texts are the surest ways to market textbooks over the long haul. I knew that I had arrived some years ago when a reviewer described *In the Beginning* as a "venerable classic." Venerable, perhaps, but I hope each edition is still vibrant and fresh!

Something on Coauthors

This book assumes that you are writing on your own, which may be true most of the time. But there are occasions, especially with textbooks, when you'll undertake a project with a coauthor, perhaps because you enjoy working together or because your interests are complementary. As archaeology becomes more specialized, more narrowly focused, coauthored texts are proliferating.

A coauthorship can be a tricky marriage, especially if there are senior and junior partners in the relationship, as often happens when an older scholar works with a less experienced colleague. The best collaborations unfold when both parties are equal partners, responsible for the same number of chapters, so that the book is a fifty-fifty enterprise. Of course, you can work with three coauthors, or divide the book sixty-forty, or whatever, but the same guidelines for the partnership apply.

Many coauthorships stumble on a lack of communication. There must be complete trust between partners and a level of communication where you can fearlessly criticize the smallest details of the other's work without incurring personal animosity. This requires some frank conversation up-front, before you even contemplate an outline. Without this level of communication, your project is bound to run into trouble.

Both parties must be fully committed to the project and to completing it on time. Unless you both work strictly to deadline, there will be inevitable problems when one half of the book is on time, but the other is delayed. This means taking a clear-eyed look at your other commitments and collectively blocking time for the project.

Right at the beginning, you need to develop a formal document in which you list precisely who is writing what, down to the individual chapter. If you are sharing a chapter, specify a lead author to mastermind each one, dividing the labor evenly. Both parties should sign this letter, which is not, of course, legally binding; think of it as a prenuptial agreement, developed as the proposal is written. Then, when you discuss the contract with the publisher, you have a previously agreed percentage split for advances, royalties, and other financial items. Don't wait until the book is written to work out sharing arrangements. I guarantee there'll be disagreements.

Intellectually, it's important that you share the same theoretical perspective and ambitions for the work, unless, of course, you're deliberately writing a book to present two contrasting perspectives.

Each author should read and thoroughly critique all the chapters, both for accuracy and to check for potential overlaps and inconsistencies. Each should also read the entire copyedit and proofs. You must also have an equal ability to write well and styles that are compatible. When submitting a proposal and specimen text, it's a good idea to send chapters written by each party, both to check that you are stylistically compatible and to demonstrate your commitment to the project.

Coauthorship is like a marriage, where you have differing interests and agreements and disagreements, but in the end you understand each other well enough to carry through the task with complete mutual trust. Obviously, it's easier if you live in the same town or within a reasonable distance, but, in these days of e-mail, you can now exchange drafts in seconds. You should make a point of sending along chapters as you write them, so that each party is right on top of the other's work. You can then react to each other's drafts and often trigger a useful intellectual exchange. But it's essential that one author alone work on the final draft to smooth out stylistic problems.

All of this may seem obvious, but it's surprising just how many co-authorships fall apart or dissolve in acrimony. It's a difficult relationship to carry off, but one that can be deeply satisfying and even lead to a series of books over the years. Having said this, I personally prefer to work alone, but I suspect that's because I've been doing it for a long time.

The Process of Textbook Writing

Like books for the trade market, writing a textbook goes through four major stages:

THE FOUR STAGES OF TEXTBOOK WRITING

■ Writing the proposal and submitting it to the publisher.

■ Writing the draft manuscript.

■ Revising it in light of the reviews obtained by the publisher.

■ Addressing production issues, which consumes much more of one's time than one might imagine.

The Proposal

While you can submit a textbook proposal over the transom to an anthropology editor, most successful ones begin with an editor suggesting that you consider writing a text, preferably on a subject of broad appeal. In making this suggestion, the editor or publisher's sales representative (who will refer you to an editor) will have decided on the basis of a face-to-face meeting that you have the enthusiasm and potential commitment to write a proposal. At an early stage, they may ask you for writing samples, so they can gauge your ability to write clearly.

The ideal textbook proposal has three parts:

■ A narrative that lays out the purpose of the book.

■ A chapter-by-chapter outline.

■ At least one specimen chapter, complete with boxes, summaries, and all other pedagogical ancillaries (the editor will suggest what's appropriate).

The narrative is far more than a statement of what your book will be about, its major themes, and its theoretical slant. Short and to the point, your proposal has to answer tough questions and be written in the clear style you will use in the book itself. What, for example, is the need for your text?

Then there's the question of competing books. What competitors are out there? How would your text be a specific improvement on them? Does it offer different coverage, a more up-to-date theoretical stance, and so on? This is the most important question for your editor: what is the niche for your book? Is there an unexploited gap in, say, the introductory method and theory market? You should be as specific as you can here.

Then you have to sell yourself. Why are you uniquely qualified to write this book? Do you have the academic and pedagogical credentials, as well as the intellectual breadth, to do so? No one expects a hagiography, but the publisher needs a profile of the author in whom they are investing.

If you're working with coauthors, be sure to specify which of you is writing each chapter.

This brings us back to the passion issue. Above all, your proposal should express an excitement—a passion—for the subject, and communicate that the subject is important to you and should also be of profound interest to your audience. Nothing resonates more clearly than enthusiasm.

The narrative leads into the chapter-by-chapter outline, which subdivides the book into parts and shows the cumulative pedagogy through the chapters, and the ancillary features such as boxes, glossaries, and so on that will accompany your narrative. Here's an example of the kind of thing you need:

Chapter 7 Rock Art

What is rock art?—its first discovery by archaeologists: Altamira, San rock art in South Africa, Lascaux—different art traditions from Stone Age Europe, Africa, and North America—recording rock art—interpreting the meaning of the art—shamans and other interpretations (with examples)—why is rock art important to the study of the past?

Boxes: Grotte de Chauvet, France; South African rock art; Chumash astronomy and art.

Note that this summary is a mixture of questions and factual coverage, designed to give a reviewer and the publisher an idea of what you will cover in this chapter. The placement of the chapter in the book should be self-evident from the subject matter that precedes and follows it.

There's no need to write the kind of narrative outline that's so important with trade proposals. Here you're concerned with showing what you are going to cover and the questions you are discussing.

The specimen chapter should be a final draft, complete with boxes, student questions, guides for further reading, and callouts for illustrations, with photocopies of the images, just as if you were submitting the final manuscript. A lot of work, you say! Of course it is, but you want to show the publisher that you know what you are talking about and that you are entirely serious and professional in your approach.

This is the stage at which you must convince yourself, your publisher, and potential reviewers that you have the academic breadth and expertise to carry off the book. For instance, some people write archaeological textbooks that are slanted heavily toward their particular expertise in Maya civilization or North America, when the subject at the introductory level is truly global. Clearly, their authors are somewhat uncomfortable in the broader academic arena of human prehistory.

The editor will review the proposal and may ask for changes at this early stage—for example, based on discussions with other instructors, there may be a subject the editors feel should be covered to better fill a particular niche. If you're lucky, these changes will not take too much time. Once the editor is happy, he or she will send out your proposal for anonymous academic review to as many as six of your colleagues, depending on the size and complexity of the book. The process can take weeks to complete and you will have to be patient. This is where trade publishing is much quicker, for there you learn your fate relatively quickly. Once the reviews are in, and if they are supportive, the editor will either come back to you for changes in light of their reports, or take the proposal as it stands to the in-house editorial board for a decision on whether to offer a contract.

Your editor won't take your proposal forward unless it has a high chance of success. If the board accepts it, they will then offer you a formal contract, complete with royalty percentages, budgets for illustrations, and an advance, typically payable in segments—on signing,

on acceptance, and on publication. These days, most textbook contracts are boilerplate agreements that have been dissected endlessly
by corporate lawyers. There is little room to negotiate away from
industry norms. Trade book contracts are heavy on boilerplate language, too, but the financial terms and advances vary considerably
from author to author, with such features as sales incentives if the
hardcover edition sells out. Yes, you hear stories of huge advances for
major textbook projects, especially when publishers are competing
for what they perceive as a hot book. When faced with such a competitive situation, never allow yourself to be seduced by ready cash.

Always choose a publisher that has its marketing sights in line and
is likely to sell your book so well that it goes into multiple editions over
many years. Steady sales performance is more important than dollars up-
front. You'll know which publishers are most effective at this from the
ways they've reached you as a potential user of their books in the past.

CRITERIA FOR SELECTING A TEXTBOOK PUBLISHER

- Does the publisher have a strong list in this area that your book
  will amplify?

- What are the house's production values? Do their books look
  cheap and hastily produced? If so, go elsewhere.

- Lastly, and most important of all, is their marketing organization
  aggressive, active in the field, and on top of the marketplace?

Development Editors

If you are writing a major text, the editor may bring a development
editor on board to work on organization and other matters. These
people are invariably helpful, especially to the first-time author. Every
text writer I've talked to who has worked with one sings their praises.
I've never had the pleasure, so can say no more.

Writing the First Draft

The worst part of writing any textbook is, of course, the first draft, a process that seems to go on forever. As with any other book, the best strategy is a fixed routine that generates 1,000 words or so a day. If you maintain this pace day after day, you can generate 6,000 or more words a week, much of an average textbook chapter. The resulting prose may be truly awful, but psychologically you are ahead of the game.

Before you start work, ask the publisher for their author's guide, and follow its instructions as far as formatting and so on from the beginning. You'll save time later.

Don't go back and revise. Plow ahead and get the entire rough draft on paper. In this way, you'll be over the mental barrier of writing the first draft and ready to look at the book as a whole. Don't worry about the content of boxes, summaries, test questions, or references. You'll think about them later on. As far as boxes are concerned, I try to identify them at first-draft stage and simply write "BOX HERE" wherever it seems appropriate to add one, and make a note of the subject matter if need be. The same thing applies to illustrations. Put a brief notation of the drawing or photograph between paragraphs where you think one is needed, and then carry on with your main narrative.

Subsequent Drafts, aka Revision

As with any other book, the essence of the final product is in the revision. This is particularly true of textbooks, which require meticulous improvement through several drafts.

The revision stage is when you disembowel your chapters, rewrite most of them completely, and end up with something approximating the final book. Some of the items you have to think about may seem startlingly arcane, but they are essential to a textbook. Here are some pointers:

Style. Keep it simple, use short sentences, and avoid passive tenses. Remember that each chapter tells a story, however mundane the subject matter. Part of the narrative flow is providing smooth links from one section to the next. A few sentences or a short paragraph can achieve this.

REVISION TASKS

■ Check that the themes and narrative flow together in a seamless whole, and make sure you have not been diverted into irrelevant detail.

■ Check for gaps, add examples if necessary, and eliminate unnecessary detail.

■ Draft boxes, questions, summaries, and other pedagogical features.

■ Add references and guides to further reading, if required and as appropriate.

■ Compile glossaries.

■ Develop the illustration program and create roughs of the line drawings.

■ Check for style, spelling, and grammar, eliminate repetition, and check for inconsistencies. Add (and check) references.

At all costs, avoid passive tenses and jargon. If you use a technical term, define it in the glossary. It's far better to oversimplify than to qualify your sentences with a clutter of "perhaps" or such ghastly phrases as "this leads us to the conclusion that." The instructor can always qualify overstatements in class if he or she desires.

Remember that a flowing, easy-to-read narrative will make your textbook stand out from the crowd.

Subheads. You will likely e-mail continually with your production editor about subheads. A logical order of such animals is essential to the reader. They divide each chapter into a transparent structure and into easily digestible, bite-size chunks.

A Typical Hierarchy of Subheads

- A-heads: major subdivisions of chapters.

- B-heads: subsections of A-head text.

- C-heads: even further subdivisions; they usually run flush to the margin.

Glossaries, definitions, etc. Textbook publishers will almost certainly require a glossary at the back of your book as an aid for students. Typically, you cross-reference the reader to the glossary by putting the term in bold in the text. You should highlight terms for the glossary as you revise the text. It's best to compile the glossary as you go along, while the subject is fresh in your mind. The publisher may ask for a list of key terms at the end of the chapter as well, along with "Questions for Discussion."

Boxes. In-text boxes break up long descriptive passages and are useful to give depth to archaeological narrative. They can cover all manner of topics—important discoveries, points of interest, key methods, even a minor tangent to the main thrust of the chapter. Most boxes are about 800 to 1,000 words long and often include a picture, the callout for which appears in the box. Three to four boxes a chapter is enough, sometimes fewer. You should work with your editor to establish the nature and function of boxes in your specific text.

Your box text should appear at the end of the chapter, with a callout in the main text indicating where the box should go:

* * * Box 1.1 goes here * * *

The production folk will move it into place as they paginate the book.

Illustrations. Now you compile your illustration program, write the legends, and add the callouts to the text. Think of the illustrations as a kind of parallel story, where you fill out details of the narrative visually, or even go off on a slight tangent. For instance, you could use a photograph of the Bronze Age Ice Man from the Italian Alps and write a legend that describes his clothing and equipment, while mentioning him only in passing in the text, with a callout to your picture. Most large archaeology textbooks are comprehensively illustrated, with up to 200 photographs or more, not counting tables and line drawings. While many of the pictures amplify the text and have the same function as boxes, others are strictly evocative or for information—maps and tables, for example.

You must also provide information on the source of each picture, and, unless the publisher is doing this, evidence that you have obtained permission to reproduce it. The publisher will give you standardized letters and information on seeking permissions. Typically, you will be asked to provide an illustration log with all the information for each picture, in the form of a spreadsheet.

Summaries, references, etc. Chapter summaries are crucial and should be written carefully, for they are what students read first, and often last. A summary covers the key points made in the chapter, mentions important examples, and notes any major conclusions drawn. Most summaries are about 250 to 300 words long.

References come in various forms, depending on the level of the text. Citations for additional student reading can appear either as "Guides to Further Reading" at the end of each chapter, or, more commonly now, on a companion web site. Such guides list major syntheses covering the subject matter of the chapter, which are both readable and contain comprehensive bibliographies. Larger texts usually have formal bibliographies, which are as much for academic use as they are for student readers. Ask your editor for guidelines on these features, which vary from house to house.

Front matter. Draft the front matter once you have a well-revised manuscript and a clear sense of the entire book. Most larger texts require two tables of contents, one a mere listing of the chapter titles, the other right down to boxes and A-heads. I have never understood why, but they do.

The preface, which is aimed as much at the instructor as the student, should be a clear statement of the goals and coverage of the book, and contains something of the rationale behind it. As previously mentioned, it's an important marketing tool, for this is what potential adopters will read. You should mention any special features of the text that set it apart and describe the pedagogical aids that accompany it. By all means add an acknowledgments section, but keep it short. The editor will add the names of the reviewers of your manuscript and their institutions. You may also require an author's note, in which you lay out conventional usages like A.D./B.C., or the use of metric measurements. Keep all the front matter short, to the point, and easy to read.

By the time you've finished these revisions, you'll probably never want to see the manuscript again. Relax, the worst is over! Print it out, then set it aside, and take a break of at least a week.

When you pick up the manuscript again, read the printout from one end to the other, checking everything from callouts and cross-references to grammar and consistency. Once you have completed this process and added your corrections to the computer file, you are ready to submit the manuscript to the publisher. (In the interests of brevity, I have omitted discussion of such supplements as instructor's guides, web pages, and so on, which are often not the concern of the text author. Your editor will brief you on requirements and your involvement.)

Review and Final Changes

While you take a well-deserved rest, your editor sends the manuscript out for academic review to between six and a dozen reviewers. The reviewer mix will include expert researchers and potential adopters of your book. This process can take several months and can be traumatic, for one's colleagues are sometimes unpleasant. The publisher uses a standard format for reviews, asking questions about the text and potential courses for which it could be adopted, but the meat is in comments and corrections. Reviews can range from the useless, even offensive, to absolutely priceless line-by-line constructive criticism.

Armed with the reviews and the editor's suggestions, you then prepare the final manuscript, without—we hope—too much major revision. If there are serious problems, be sure to talk to your editor at length before attempting any rewrites.

Once the revisions are completed and approved by the publisher, you can relax for a few weeks as the book is released for production.

Production

As with a trade work, your editor now steps into the background, as a production editor or group is assigned to your book. Much of this team may now be based offshore, even on the other side of the world. Remember that at this stage you're a member of a team working on your book, all of whom are operating to strict timetables. Expect to be bombarded by questions about inconsistencies, missing references in the bibliography or glossary, and so on. You will endear yourself to everyone by answering promptly and meeting deadlines.

The production process follows that for any book. Particularly with a complicated manuscript like a textbook, the copyedit assumes profound importance. As with any other book, assume that the copy editor knows what he or she is doing, and only argue over the really important issues (if there are any). The remarks about copyediting in Chapter 8 apply with equal force here.

At some point, you'll be asked to approve the drafts of the line drawings and tables. You may also find yourself working with a photo researcher, if the publisher is assuming responsibility for obtaining the images you suggest.

Photo researchers are true experts on visual sources of all kinds. They have encyclopedic knowledge of photographic agencies and their specialties, and of the intricacies of obtaining permissions to reproduce pictures. With luck, your book will be assigned to a researcher with at least some background in anthropology and archaeology, who will know which agencies and institutions specialize in your subject matter. For instance, Art Resource, Corbis, and Photo Researchers are agencies with large archaeology holdings, many of them of artifacts in museums. The researcher will know which institutions give slow service, or never answer requests, and so on. His or her knowledge is specialized and invaluable. The secret is to be flexible in your requirements. Normally, for each picture you'll receive a selection of images to choose among, unless you have specified the precise picture and source. It often happens that your choice of image is simply not available, so have viable alternatives at the ready. I have found photo researchers to be intelligent, perceptive people who are a pleasure to deal with.

Months after you've approved the proofs, the advance copy of your book arrives and it all seems worth it. Then there's silence, except for the inevitable nitpicking e-mails from people who delight in pointing out the grievous error on page 86 but almost invariably never write books themselves. My favorite was an anonymous correspondent who sent me a photocopied page with a line alongside a single paragraph with the enigmatic comment "wrong." Mercifully, there is mostly silence as the marketplace absorbs your book.

The only formal feedback you will probably get will come from your editor and from your biannual royalty statement. But I urge you to encourage comments from colleagues and students whenever you encounter people who are using, or have used, your book. You'll probably receive frank appraisals you would never have expected, like that from a student who wrote to me pointing out that a table was wrongly placed in *In the Beginning*—a glaring error missed by the editors and me, and all other users. I quietly corrected the error in the next edition and wondered just how thoroughly people read textbooks! A great deal of feedback comes via e-mail: I publish my e-mail address at the end of the preface for that purpose, with a note encouraging users to contact me.

Revised Editions

If the book does well, you'll find yourself on a three- or four-year revision cycle, dictated not only by sales but by the number of unsold books returned by stores and the market in second-hand copies. Used texts are a huge business, which has no financial benefit to either the author or the publisher. Textbook publishers defend themselves against declining sales by putting popular books on three- to four-year revision cycles. If you write a widely used text, you are sentenced to the regular treadmill of revised editions.

Revisions are not a lovely experience, but they are part of serious textbook writing. In fact, don't take on a text unless you're prepared to factor in time for revisions, which have to be completed by fixed deadlines. All revisions are governed by the selling season, which is the winter and spring, so your revised edition has to appear in time for the sales period. This means that your revised manuscript will have to be in-house on a specified date; otherwise it will be late and you will lose sales.

Unlike many of the sciences, archaeology is a comparatively slow-moving subject, which means that many of one's revisions are relatively minor—changes to illustrations and maps, adding new discoveries, correcting errors, discussing new theoretical perceptions, and so on—but there's no excuse for not taking a close look at the entire book. Cumulatively, the changes add up, so a minor revision is subtly different from its predecessor.

Major revisions require considerable time, months rather than weeks. They occur about every second or third iteration as your book goes through multiple editions. The second edition is normally a heavy revision, where you benefit from the feedback and track record from the first one. With major revisions, you can expect to change 40 percent of the text or more and to make major modifications to the illustrations.

Revisions depend on both your own perceptions of the changing archaeological world and feedback from others. I make a point of maintaining revision files for each textbook, where I keep potential material for future editions. Informal feedback from colleagues and students is invaluable and comes in all the time. Your editor will also have ideas on how the book can be improved, based on his or her travels to campuses and conferences. He or she may want to add new pedagogical features, additional illustrations, or reduce the length of the text. All these suggestions will be market driven. Your editor will also have commissioned reviews of the previous edition from people who have used it and people who have not. These will help guide your revision from various perspectives, among them classroom use of the book, student perceptions, and an academic viewpoint. Note that the preface is particularly important in revised editions, for it is here that you spell out the specific changes and improvements that you have made. As we've already said, prospective adopters read prefaces to find out what's new.

The actual work of revision proceeds from an electronic version of the previous edition sent you by the publisher, together with copies of the book itself, so that you can use them to compile the new illustration program.

Textbook writing is far from glamorous, and cannot, by any stretch of the imagination, be described as fun. But a successful text brings with it a profound sense of gratification and the thought that you may be doing something to change public perceptions of archaeology in the future.

NOW THAT YOU'VE FINISHED
YOUR DISSERTATION . . .

*Rule 10: Take a deep breath and take your time
deciding what to do.*

S O YOU'VE FINALLY FILED your dissertation, deposited a bound copy in the library, and have received your doctorate. Congratulations and good luck in finding a fulfilling job! One thing is certain. You've barely begun writing.

Having reached this critical point in your burgeoning research career, you now face some challenging and strategic professional decisions surrounding your dissertation. At this particular moment you probably never want to see it again—ever. But the mood will pass and you'll begin thinking about what lies ahead. Your thesis will play an important part in your short-term future and career planning, especially if you are lucky enough to land a tenure-track position at a research university.

The next step in a ladder faculty career is tenure, which guarantees you permanent employment until retirement age. Typically, a tenure evaluation begins after about six to eight years. This elaborate process requires not only your own self-evaluation, but extramural letters, a vote by your department, and a formal decision by a campus-wide tenure committee comprised of faculty members from a range of disciplines. At a research university, your publication record is of paramount importance. And this is where writing and your dissertation come in. The decisions you make about your thesis now can have a direct bearing on your chances of being awarded tenure years down the line. So from this point onward, you need to think hard about how you publish your doctoral work.

The Realities of Your Dissertation

It's surprising just how how many newly minted PhDs believe that their dissertation can be turned into a book with just a few months of work. Nothing could be further from the truth. A doctoral dissertation is a specialized piece of research written to satisfy your committee that you have mastered your field of specialty and have made an original contribution to it. In the final analysis, it's a demonstration of competence, sometimes brilliant, often good but not outstanding, and sometimes downright mediocre. In making decisions about what to do with this demonstration of competence, you need to have absolutely no illusions about your research abilities, the importance of your work to the field, and your writing abilities. A lack of such illusions, and a dispassionate eye, are powerful weapons in your decision-making. Let's look at some key questions.

The Questions

Do I really want to continue work on this same project, or start something new? You may be tired of, say, environmental evidence for climate change in the early Mississippian and have a chance to work on the implications of Maya lake cores. Do you want to break out, try something new, and then return to your Mississippian materials in, say, a couple of years? The decision involves far more than weariness, for almost all dissertations can be improved after a couple of years. By then, you'll have more feedback from a wider range of colleagues than merely the three or four members of your committee. So when you are ready to publish, you will do so with a greater maturity and clearer understanding of your material. No, I am not insulting you. All good researchers grow and their material grows with them. There are significant benefits in taking your time to publish your work. This is especially the case if you have published some papers before submitting your thesis, which is now a common practice.

Papers or a book? The old saying that tenure requires a book still has much truth, but by no means all committees are that rigid. In these days of multidisciplinary research, huge amounts of specialized research appear in peer-reviewed journals, just as they do in the sciences. This is certainly true with much narrowly focused research on such topics as isotope analysis. Your chances of receiving tenure from an impressive portfolio of peer-reviewed papers in national and international journals are now much better than they were a generation ago. Much depends on the nature of your research.

Another major consideration revolves around your dissertation topic. If your thesis is basically a site monograph or a stage-by-stage description of an important archaeological excavation, you are clearly in the business of writing a major narrative with numerous sub-narratives. In such cases—my dissertation was a good example—a book is hands-down the best way to go. (For the curious, the book is *Iron Age Cultures in Northern Rhodesia:* Volume 1: *Kalomo and Kangila* [London: Chatto and Windus, 1967]—Enjoy!) If, on the other hand, the chapters of your dissertation are concerned with separate incidents of analysis or highly technical, rather narrow topics that collectively form a larger picture, you are almost certainly better off publishing them as a series of papers in refereed journals—for example, in *The Journal of Anthropological Archaeology.* And, eventually, when you are ready, and if the research merits it, you can then submit a synthesis of your research and its wider implications to an outlet like *Antiquity* or *American Antiquity.* If you are careful, you can assemble a nice portfolio of refereed articles over a few years that will do much to impress a promotion committee. Avoid, however, the trap of publishing the same basic article in several journals. That's resumé padding and is easily detected, especially by colleagues. (For journal articles and submitting them, see Chapter 11.)

More on books. If you elect to go the book route, realize that it can take two years or more to get your book accepted, let alone published, in these days of declining publishers' budgets. This is after you have spent a large amount of time completely rewriting most of your thesis to make it a marketable book. Aren't you sick of it already? Recall what we said about proposal writing and publishers' decisions in Chapter 4. The comments in that chapter apply as much to academic books as they do to trade works. *Remember: your final book manuscript is something completely different from your dissertation.* The book route is higher risk—although, of course, it's a no-brainer if you have a truly unique piece of research. Anthropologist Richard Lee's dissertation research on the !Kung San of the Kalahari Desert in southern Africa had publishers slavering—and with good reason. The resulting book is now a classic.

Whatever you do, develop a well thought-out writing plan and stick to it. In the final analysis, in this day and age you are probably better off mining your dissertation for articles than a book. Then, as these contributions appear and your research interests mature, you can take on a project that will be planned from the beginning to result in a book.

On Mentors

If you are lucky, you had a faculty mentor who guided your doctoral work and who evolved from an instructor into a valued colleague. All too many PhD students never acquire a mentor. I never did, something I shall regret to the end of my days. It took years to catch up. When you graduate and get a job, you still need a mentor, which is why it's critically important to develop close working relationships with colleagues, especially more senior scholars with interests related to yours. Such relationships are more valuable than rubies and can last for decades. As time goes on, they become partnerships of equals, especially if the senior partner has the sense to realize that you may know more about some things than he or she does. And, very often, you are right and they are proven wrong.

Cultivating a mentor is a matter of mutual respect, of seeking advice and taking and giving criticism while leaving your egos outside the door. Mentors are more than friends. True mentoring partnerships stem from relationships based on respect for each other and for the field and should last a long time. I've had invaluable advice about research strategies, about publication opportunities, journal submissions, fund-raising, and all the myriad aspects of being a researcher and a teacher. As you become older and more experienced, you tend to become the senior mentor, bringing criticism but, above all, opportunities to the relationship. This is one of the most satisfying rewards of being a researcher, especially in today's world, where so much fieldwork and laboratory inquiry is carried out by teams rather than individuals— the old syndrome of great, larger-than-life archaeologists.

Seek out mentors, then become a mentor. Life after the dissertation will be so much more satisfying—and your writing will improve, too.

Now on to Writing . . .

With these preliminaries out of the way, let's take a closer look at the general principles of writing for an academic audience. The remarks that follow are by way of the preliminaries. We look at the anatomy of articles, academic books, and edited volumes in Chapter 11.

Let's start with a paraphrase of a remark by the legendary Gordon Willey, doyen of American archaeologists: "Good writing is good writing. It is nothing else." Willey was discussing archaeology and its relationship to anthropology. I'm talking about writing for academic audiences. We archaeologists suffer from a disadvantage in that we have no tradition of distinguished writing in academic archaeology, something that historians have long encouraged, albeit with mixed results.

Most professional archaeologists learn how to write papers in graduate school, which is hardly an ideal environment for doing so, given the many other pressures involved in preparing a seminar paper. Unfortunately, relatively few professors spend much time critiquing their students' writing, in part because they were never taught how to write clearly themselves. Furthermore, the genre known as academic writing seems to operate on a well-tried formula that is more concerned with perpetuating a stylistic status quo than clear exposition.

The Cambridge archaeologist Grahame Clark was right when he said that he could tell if an article was worth reading in the first two pages (see Chapter 6). I asked him how. "Clarity of style and clear objectives," he replied succinctly. These are two fundamental hallmarks of good academic writing.

Many academics, even journal editors, seem to think that the best papers are those cloaked in jargon and conditioned obscurity. Wrong! Stellar academic writing has an elegance and clarity of argument, description, and exposition that makes it a pleasure to read. Unfortunately, most academic writing never achieves this level. Suffice it to say that there are colleagues whose writing I always look forward to reading and others whose writings I avoid unless they are compellingly important and essential. Among the latter are some of my own contributions. I shudder when I read some of my early papers:

> Smoking is attested by the presence of a pair of pipe tongs, and fourteen fragments. (Fagan 1961:230)

Compare this monstrosity with the following from a recent paper on archaeology in highland Bolivia:

> Paul Connerton begins his book *How Societies Remember* with the sentence: "All beginnings contain an element of recollection", creating new out of old. . . . His thesis focuses on the central importance of commemoration and bodily practice in building and maintaining society while forming social identities. (Roddick and Hastorf 2010:157)

This clear exposition of the importance of tradition led me further into the paper. If I were reading my now (fortunately) long out-of-date paper on Central African ironwork, I would go elsewhere as soon as possible. Fortunately, some good writer-mentors took me in hand.

Writing an academic article, chapter, or paper for the first time is a daunting prospect, but it can be immeasurably easier if you lay down some simple principles for yourself:

Tell a story. As I emphasized in Chapter 1, your responsibility as a writer, academic or not, is to lead the reader through what you have to

FAGAN'S ACADEMIC WRITING MANTRAS

■ Tell a story.

■ Keep sentences short.

■ Avoid passive tenses.

■ Eschew unnecessary jargon.

■ Steer clear of clichés.

■ Strive for simple, economic clarity

say. Every paper, be it about an obscure pottery type or a sensational fossil hominin, tells a story, however minute, however important. You are a storyteller just like a popular writer, with the difference that you have to show that your approach is original and that you are using primary data (unless, of course, you are writing a broad literature synthesis). Write your paper around a story line and it will be immeasurably easier to complete. Here's a recent example by an author who is well aware of the importance of storytelling in a technical paper: "Stone tools are products of past human societies, but what can they tell us about the nature of these societies and their symbolic conventions—their ideals, beliefs, and values?" (Brumm 2010:179). Adam Brumm goes on to describe the symbolic and cosmological associations of a greenstone axe quarry in Australia. From the beginning, we know where he is going. Give your paper or chapter a story line.

Keep sentences short. Yesterday, I caught myself writing the following:

> Dams were inevitable as agribusiness expanded and the technology to build them of concrete emerged early in the twentieth century. An era of aggressive federal reclamation and dam projects began with the passage of the Newlands Act in 1902 and a boom in irrigation agriculture was soon under way. Congress set up a Colorado River Commission 20 years later and its members hammered out

the Colorado River Compact, which allocated water between the seven states that shared the Colorado River Basin. (Early draft of Fagan in press)

I caught myself tolerating a horrible beginning to a paragraph, with too many "ands." The obvious potentially shorter sentences ran on, one into the other. Once I removed two of the three "ands," the flow was much better, the historical points were made, and the paragraph became infinitely more readable.

Many instances of obfuscatory academic writing stem from undue reliance on long sentences—and even paragraphs, for that matter. This is because the writer is anxious to avoid disturbing a train of thought as he or she puts it on the screen. A great deal of revision time should revolve around sentence and paragraph structure (see Chapter 7).

Avoid passive tenses. Passive tenses are the curse of academic writing. Why did I write "It was expected that some sequential change in the proportions of decorative types . . . would be observable" in a discussion of an African pottery sequence, when I could have written: "We expected to observe some changes in decorative styles over time?" (Fagan, Phillipson, and Daniels 1969:44). Why did I write this horrible sentence? Youthful naïveté and inexperience, I suspect, and I shudder today. Yes, passive tenses have their place, but the more you remain in the active voice, the clearer your message will come across.

As much as possible, eschew jargon. We have become addicted to jargon, often the more obscure the better. Much of the excess flourishes in the theoretical literature, where some writers have even added glossaries to their books and papers. Of course, you need to use some technical terms, such as "Acheulian" or familiar labels for pottery styles in the Midwest. These have specific meanings to fellow specialists. In general, however, you should use as little jargon as possible. When you do, be guided by the principle of communicating in terms that are commonly used by your colleagues. Never insert jargon just to show that you are aware of a specialist term or introduce new terms when they are unnecessary. And, please, don't try to prove you are learned by calling, for example, rabbits "lagomorphs" or cats "passerines." A rabbit is a rabbit is a rabbit. Keep it simple, clear, and technically correct.

Avoid cliché expressions. Again, I sinned: "The archaeological evidence outlined above enables us to conclude that the economy of the Ingombe Ilede people . . ." (Fagan, Phillipson, and Daniels 1969:90). Pomposity reigned. How much better to have written: "The Ingombe Ilede people relied on subsistence agriculture, cattle and small stock, also hunting and foraging." It's obvious that this statement's based on archaeological evidence. Shun cliché expressions like "This leads to the conclusion that" or "Other evidence also points to." The words "suggests that" should be expunged from your writing vocabulary. A perceptive reader will know that you've used these phrases because you are at a loss for a decent sentence. Again, revision pays off. This is Chapter 7 stuff.

Above all, strive for simple, economic clarity. This should be self-evident but all too often is not. Keep to the point, make it engaging, and do not go on too long. Before you start writing, acquire a copy of Strunk and White's *Elements of Style* and remember its admonitions, among them:

> Vigorous writing is concise. A statement should contain no unnecessary words, a paragraph no unnecessary sentences. . . . This requires not that the writer make his sentences short, or that he avoid all detail and treat his subjects only in outline, but that every word should tell. (Strunk and White 2008 [1972]: ix–x)

With these principles in mind, we can look more closely at academic article and book writing in Chapter 11.

ACADEMIC WRITING

Rule 11: Above all, write clear, vigorous prose.

S OONER OR LATER, ANYONE engaged in archaeological research has to write up their investigations for their colleagues, whether for an academic project or a CRM investigation. You may have started this process before completing a PhD, but whenever you start, you're engaged in the enterprise of academic writing, be it a paper, a book chapter, or a book. This chapter covers the basics of such writing.

Academic Articles

The audience for any academic writing is a group of your well-informed peers. There are also occasional readers with a casual interest in the subject matter, perhaps for a synthesis or for teaching purposes. Students may also use your work for their research. Writing an article or book for a general audience requires that you both entertain and inform your readers, while explaining what is often a complex subject in clear, jargon-free terms. By contrast, with a specialist readership, all of this, at least in theory, goes overboard. Or does it? In my view, clear, vivid writing is as important in a purely academic paper as it is in the most popular of works. Why? Because your task is to present your research in a readable way, so that both peer reviewers (of whom more anon) and your readers understand that you are making an original contribution to the field. In short, like a popular author, you are in the business of telling a story.

The prospect of submitting an article about your research can be very daunting, for you often believe that your topic is neither significant nor original. Realize that not every article becomes a classic or is widely quoted. In most cases, you'll certainly add some new ideas or insights to a body of existing debate and information, even if they are not earthshakingly important. Your responsibility as an archaeologist dealing with finite data is to publish your research in an appropriate outlet, so that others are aware of it and can use it.

ACADEMIC PAPERS: QUESTIONS YOU SHOULD ASK YOURSELF

Instead of worrying about significance, focus your mind on a series of relevant questions:

- Do you have one or two interesting ideas, fresh data, or a new analytical method?

- Have you presented your data and ideas in a seminar or at a professional meeting? If so, what was the audience reaction and feedback?

- Have you shared your material with close colleagues with similar specialties? What was their reaction? Are they colleagues with significant publication experience?

- Can you describe the content of your article and the points it makes in a few sentences? Does your paper, if drafted or in your head, cover these details?

If you can answer all these questions, you are on your way.

Once you have decided to write your paper, many of the routines described in other chapters of this book apply. Just as if you were writing a book or popular article, you need to develop a comprehensive outline, then draft the text—the 1,000 words a day formula works just as well here—and then revise, revise, and revise (see Chapters 6 and 7).

Choosing an Outlet

At this early stage, you should have a clear idea what journal you are planning to target. In this era of extreme specialization, new journals proliferate like rabbits, many of them published only on the Web or for tiny niche audiences. Selecting the right journal for your paper requires careful thought and an informed reading of likely journals. Resist the temptation to submit your first paper to a major international or national journal. Chances are that it is too specialized; such journals tend to accept articles that have wider appeal, or at least broader methodological or theoretical significance than your first effort is likely to possess. My first contribution was published in the *Proceedings of the Dorset Archaeological Society*, was only of local interest, and is now deservedly forgotten except as an antiquarian curiosity. It's pointless, also, to submit an article to, say, the *Plains Anthropologist* when your research covers another area or is, at best, of peripheral interest to the journal's readers. Take careful account of your specialty, say, quantitative archaeology in the Southwest, or Mississippian ritual, and focus your efforts on journals that are most likely to be interested in your work. Look at the journals you have cited in your work as some gauge of which ones might be appropriate. At one blow, you'll improve your chances of acceptance immeasurably. By the same token, create a list of second and third preferences in case your first choice rejects the article.

As part of your selection process, read a variety of articles from recent issues, in addition to the editorial guidelines. Does the editor specify criteria for articles? Are there word limits? It's pointless to submit a 9,000-word article to a journal that accepts contributions that are limited to 6,000 words. What are the policies on illustrations and photographs? Do you have to provide a subsidy for publication—as is the case with some journals in the sciences? By all means send a query letter to the editor, giving specific details of what you are writing about. Obviously, the editor won't accept the article sight unseen or without peer review but will at least give you an idea whether it fits within the guidelines for that journal. Colleagues with experience publishing in different journals may also be able to give you valuable insights. If they have some connections with a journal, they may be able to "introduce" you, which will also increase your chances of success. Above all, don't have delusions of grandeur. Multi-authored articles or letters to *Nature* or *Science* are all very prestigious and research institutions love them, but an article written by yourself alone is far more career enhancing, and personally satisfying, than merely being a name in a long string of authors. Whatever journal you choose for your submission, what really counts are original approaches, new data, and evidence that the article is a significant contribution to the field.

Peer Review

"Peer-reviewed papers" have become the equivalent of sacrifices to the academic gods. An accepted paper in a peer-reviewed journal has become a sort of intellectual cachet. Peer review at its best can be a healthy exercise, *provided* that the editor chooses conscientious reviewers. Often they will ask you to provide the names of some potential reviewers; offer to do so if they don't ask. Typically, a peer review involves up to half a dozen scholars, most commonly two or three, whose reports come to you anonymously, with a summary and comments from the editor. These can be enormously helpful, even reviews by people who disagree with you, for they may have perspectives that you have overlooked. What are unhelpful and regrettably more common than you might think are reviews written by colleagues with agendas, intellectual axes to grind, or set positions that they perceive as being threatened by your paper. Fortunately, good editors will help you navigate through such minefields, and, of course, you have the right to reject anything you wish, provided that you can support your rejections in specific terms. It's not uncommon for reviewers to disagree with you and with one another. I once had six reviewers of an article who all disagreed with one another and with me—but the paper was revised and published.

More important, in almost all cases it is the journal editor who makes the final decision on your paper. The editor has the right to over-rule reviewer comments and accept your paper, or reject it even if the reviews are glowing. Thus, discuss with the editor what he or she wants you to do to the paper based on the reviews. Confirm your agreed-upon changes with the editor in writing at that time, and when you submit a revised draft, highlight what you have and have not done on that list.

Peer reviewing is a clumsy and often lengthy process that can take many months, but usually it's worth the wait. Some journals, notably the British journal *Antiquity*, pride themselves on a quick turn-around, but you should realize that they turn down a lot of papers because they are more appropriate for more specialized journals.

The Anatomy of an Academic Paper

Regrettably, a formula for academic papers has evolved over the years, which results in an often mind-numbing similarity in format and presentation in journal issue after journal issue. The formula goes somewhat like this: preliminary statement – literature survey – presentation of theoretical arguments and hypothesis – presentation of data – analysis – conclusions – acknowledgments and references. This is somewhat of a straitjacket, which does not, of course, work for all kinds of archaeological papers, so you need to use this framework in a very flexible manner. Still, many journal editors, and even more reviewers, expect to see an article presented in the standard format. Unless there is a good reason to deviate from the norm, take the conservative route and the standard outline.

Simple Rules

Whatever format you choose, please do the following:

- **Keep the style simple and no-nonsense**, without any elaborate literary flourishes or evocative descriptions. You are writing not for a general audience but for informed colleagues. This does not mean that you need to espouse a "dense," convoluted style and paper structure.

Your purpose is to educate and advance knowledge, but there is nothing wrong with a nice style that charms the reader.

■ **Show respect for others.** Remember that the message of your paper is more than purely intellectual. You are writing as a member of a relatively small scientific community, who deserve your courtesy and respect.

■ **Eschew emotion.** *Never* engage in ad-hominem invective or attacks on a scholar with competing ideas to your own. In the end, you are probably both partially correct. Never be patronizing, or demean yourself by trying to score points. Such approaches are counterproductive.

■ **Never say that your research was not worth the time and effort that went into it.** It's surprising how often people do this. And, by the same token, don't engage in triumphalism or boasting if your analysis turns out flawlessly. It's sobering, but true: much of your research will be disproved by later work, perhaps generations later. At least 60 percent of the field research I carried out four decades ago has been shown to be wrong, or at least partially wrong. Humility never does any harm.

GUIDES FOR WRITING ABOUT DATA

■ Brevity and economic use of adjectives make for clear description.

■ Short paragraphs, active tenses, and brief sentences work best.

■ Be specific about details, including measurements.

■ Put as much quantitative detail into tables as possible.

■ Illustrate only when absolutely necessary, but when it is, do it well.

Whatever the subject matter of your paper, you'll have to break it down into component parts, even if the components vary from one subject matter or journal to another. What follows are some general comments, following the widely used formula mentioned above.

Title, Abstract, and Keywords

Decide on your title and write your abstract right at the beginning, before you do anything else. These are, surprisingly enough, some of the most important elements of your paper.

Trade publishers spend a lot of time on titles. So should you. What is your paper about? You need to identify this. How can you attract attention to your paper through the title? Again, this is an important consideration. A quote sometimes works, so does a catchy phrase. "Soli ironworking in Central Africa" does not exactly pique interest. But "The Rape of the Nile" does. You get the general idea.

Titles attract web crawlers, especially if they are accompanied by telling, distinctive keywords. As you write your abstract, then your paper, compile a list of keywords, from which you'll select four or five that really stand out. In the case of *The Rape of the Nile*, one might choose "Egyptology," "tomb robbing," "great archaeological discoveries," or "mummies." You certainly wouldn't choose "archaeology, history of" unless you want to draw a strictly academic audience. As we'll see in Chapter 12, keywords and tags are a basic way of attracting readers to your work. Choose those words carefully.

Abstracts are equally important for attracting attention. Most journals require an abstract of some 250 words or so. As you write this, be sure to include keywords. These comprise your promise to the reader of what they will learn from the article. Then make sure that you deliver. Arrange for foreign language translations of the abstract where appropriate and specified.

The Introduction

Your introduction should be short and sweet, a simple statement of the problem and of the objectives of your research. A "hook" in scientific writing is very different from that in a popular forum. Here your introduction lays out the objectives of your research and your article up-front. This enables the reader to decide whether your contribution is relevant to his or her specific interests. Your audience has but one question: what original contribution does your article make? Your introduction should also identify the site or area you are working in and its precise location.

Literature Review

Avoid wearisome recitations of references. Your review should build on your introduction and be framed in the context of specific questions. What, simply put, have others done? Here you list only the most important, basic references. For instance, when writing about the first Americans, you could say: "General surveys of the first settlement of the Americas have proliferated in recent years. Meltzer (2009) provides a definitive summary and comprehensive references." Then go on to narrow the focus: "However, as Meltzer points out, the literature on the first settlement of coastal British Columbia is still very sparse, the latest review being that of . . . ." You have set the stage and can now zero in on your project and its significance to wider debates about first settlement.

Now that you're narrowed down, you proceed to review very briefly previous investigations of your site or area, the finds made, and the analytical conclusions drawn. Again, be brief and to the point, ending up with a clear statement as to how your research seeks to solve problems identified by earlier workers, or builds on their fieldwork or analysis.

Theoretical Argument and Research Design

At this point, you've introduced the reader to your project, your location, and the literature. Now it's time to write a short section on your theoretical approach. Here again, you need to draw on earlier research, using it to create your own theoretical framework and hypotheses. End this section with a brief account of your research design, as this will serve to lead into the presentation of your data.

Presenting the Data

Before setting anything on the computer or compiling a single table or graph, ask yourself the following questions and set your answers down as jotted notes:

- What categories of my data are absolutely relevant and essential to the objectives of my paper?

- What categories may be useful but should be kept on one side in case they are needed?

- What data need to be summarized in tables or graphs to accompany the paper? How do I keep this to a minimum and present the material effectively?

- What format, other than that of my printed article, am I going to use to make all my data, including site records, available to later researchers as a permanent record? CD, web page, hard copy? How am I going to cross-reference this material to my paper, so that other researchers can access it easily in years to come and on a permanent basis?

Do all this right at the beginning, for it allows you to reduce your data down to a manageable size. Forget what you may have done in your doctoral dissertation, which was to set down everything in tables and discuss each one, or most of them, in detail. Here you are writing a paper about a specific aspect of your work. It could, for example, be about porpoise bones or watercraft, lithic technology or changing house plans. Whatever your research problem, you need to organize your data as economically and simply as possible, however complex it is in the raw. Your data is the supporting actor to your intellectual script.

I strongly urge you to organize and finalize as many tables and graphs as you need, first. Then you know what to highlight in the text. And make sure that your narrative interprets the data, rather than just repeating it. In other words, get your data in order before writing a word.

When presenting your data, your writing requires directness and precision, fueled by clear thinking. You must never bog the reader down in excessive detail or use unnecessarily complicated descriptions. When writing descriptive prose, you need to adopt a mind-set that focuses on pure description, not analysis. You may be describing an excavation strategy or a stratigraphic profile, a storage pit, or a small assemblage of stone artifacts. Here you work with detail, on minor differences in artifact form or style, on colors, design motifs, or seemingly trivial information about the placement of hearthstones or the extent of minor occupation layers.

Paragraphs and sentence structure are of prime importance when writing descriptive prose. Paragraphs are really the reader's signposts through your data. Each should have a specific purpose. On occasion, I have written a draft and then, before revising, annotated each paragraph with the question it is supposed to answer. This works well if not carried too far. I've found that shorter paragraphs work best when writing about data, but don't hesitate to make them longer *if* the subject demands it. A new one should indicate a change in subject within the overall plot of your description, such that a reader could make an outline of your data section from your paragraphs—as you should have done. They set the order and logic of the data presentation. What is a short paragraph in this context? I counted some of my paragraphs and found that the shorter ones were about 200 to 300 words, with longer ones lying in the 300- to 400-word range. A paragraph stands alone, yet it's important that you link one to the next, to provide the reader with continuity, which is an important element of good data presentation. (This paragraph is just about 200 words, but I think it's covered the ground—and Mitch Allen thinks it's just the right length, too!)

The word "continuity" implies a flowing narrative that connects all parts of the story, whatever it is, in a seamless way. (There, we've bridged the previous paragraph to this one!) I always find linking paragraphs, indeed entire sections of an article or chapter, one of the harder things to achieve successfully. There are commonplace ways to do this, such as using phrases like "furthermore," "however," "nevertheless," and so on, but these are easily overused and can quickly degenerate into ghastly floaters like "This leads us to the conclusion that . . ." which pollute countless pages of academic prose. The best way to achieve continuity is to introduce the subject of the following paragraph in the last sentence of the previous one. Do this in a natural way, as I did a few moments ago. I used the word "continuity," which is the subject of this paragraph. There are many ingenious ways of doing this easily, usually within a single sentence.

Every paragraph consists of several sentences. Pay careful attention to sentence structure and to length. Above all, strive to keep them relatively short. Make sure that you don't prolong the sentence again and again, with the result that the reader finds him- or herself frantically wondering when it will end and the story will move on, but it never seems to as the phrases keep on proliferating. This horrible sentence has 53 words and is an abomination. What about this instead: "There's no fixed word length, but avoid stringing the reader along. It's easy to add phrase after phrase, leaving the reader wondering when you'll move on." Same material, more succinct treatment: this is much easier to read. The other extreme is, of course, the machine-gun-like staccato sentences beloved of some novel writers.

Your most powerful weapon in sentence composition is punctuation, which is an art unto itself, especially the judicious use of commas and semicolons. The only way to learn punctuation is to practice it, armed with a copy of the *Chicago Manual of Style*—a bible, like Strunk and White, for all serious writers. It's worth pointing out that no two writers punctuate the same way, so don't despair! All publishers use professional copy editors, who will go over your manuscript and correct little technical punctuation errors that you didn't get right in high school English class.

Simple paragraphs, simple sentences, and simple words: these should be your mantras, whether writing description or argument. We inhabit a discipline that seems to love obscure words and borrows them promiscuously from other fields, such ghastly words as "heuristic," "reflexive," and so on. I must confess that the moment I read such obscurities, my eyes glaze over. Even worse, such words can become fashionable and part of the archaeological vocabulary, to the point that archaeologists seem compelled to use them. Ask yourself a simple question. When you use a word like "heuristic," what do you mean? Will your readers understand either the word or why you are using it? As I said earlier, eschew jargon if you possibly can, even at the risk of being unfashionable. Using such phrases may seem impressive, but when such words proliferate, archaeological prose becomes ever more obfuscatory and deadly. "I have argued that more material entanglement and objectification lead to faster change" (Hodder 2006:258). What does this mean?

Your data section should be coherent, flow easily from one paragraph to the next, and present an easily followed story, or rather data sequence, which forms the basis for your analysis. Here, every word in a sentence tells.

Discussion

The discussion section moves from description to argument. Here you state your case, based on your data. Argumentative writing comes in many forms, typically involving both the presentation and interpretation of new evidence and the examination of earlier research. Your analysis may not be very long—perhaps 1,500 words or so—but it must have a central argument and ideas as its spine. With relatively few words to play with, taut, well-organized writing with a deliberate structure is essential, to the point that your end point arrives back where you began. Your analysis should end by broadening your focus away from your own research. This is the section of the paper that will receive the closest scrutiny from your colleagues, as will the conclusions that follow.

Conclusions

The conclusions follow on from the analysis and should summarize your main points and arguments. Here you need to answer wider questions. What contribution does this research make to, say, our understanding of the first settlement of British Columbia at the end of the Ice Age? What important questions does the project raise that amplify earlier research, or even prove it wrong? Are there new methodological or theoretical advances that need highlighting? Finally, you need a brief and *specific* statement on what kinds of future research will be beneficial.

References and Acknowledgments

I strongly urge you to compile your reference list as you go along. Not only will this save a great deal of work later on, but you will also guard against duplication. Keep references to an efficient minimum. As I noted earlier, there's no need to cite everything. And be sure to conform to the guidelines for references, web pages, and so on that were laid out by the journal of your choice. And, please, do not cite PhD dissertations. They are unpublished data and are usually accessible only on microfilm, if there. The old rule applies in archaeology. Unpublished data are scientifically inaccessible and therefore useless. Believe it or not, there are many of us who simply copy reference lists from other papers, references that we have never read. Please don't be this stupid. You'll get caught out soon enough.

People set a big store on acknowledging everyone's help. Again, keep it short and be careful to acknowledge funding sources. There is no need to mention all the people who helped you, especially mentors and reviewers.

Once You Have a Draft . . . .

This book has many litanies. One of them is "revise, revise, revise." This applies with equal force to academic papers. As part of the revision process, be sure to ask a few close colleagues to read a draft. Their insights will be invaluable and sometimes save you from grievous errors. You should acknowledge their assistance in the acknowledgments. Apart from anything else, it means that they will (usually) not be asked to peer review the article—and the reader will know who has read it before publication.

Before submitting, be sure to check the spelling, and not only with a spell checker. You should also double-check all the measurements, giving metric or imperial measurements where specified. It's amazing how many nitpickers come out of the woodwork with measurement corrections. After some of the e-mails I receive, I conjure up images of people peering line by line at one's work, obsessing about meters and feet.

Once everything is ready and carefully checked, you are ready to submit the article in whatever form the journal editor requires, whether in hard copy or electronically. A cover letter is appropriate, but keep it brief, indicating exactly what you are submitting in terms of drawings, photographs, computer CDs, and so on. Do not describe your paper in the letter. That's the abstract's job.

Academic Books

Scholarly Books

The archaeologist-turned-academic publisher Robin Derricourt has written *An Author's Guide to Scholarly Publishing*, an admirable book about publishing books with university presses and other publishers who specialize in scholarly work (see "Resources for Writers" at the end of this book). Written in the form of letters to hypothetical potential authors, it is a gem of priceless information on what to do and not to do. Like this book, and Graham Connah's volume *Writing about Archaeology* (again, see "Resources for Writers"), Derricourt stresses the importance of clarity and fluent writing. He also emphasizes careful research into publishing houses before you submit your proposal, for many of them also specialize. For instance, the University of Alaska Press is unlikely to be very interested in Southwestern archaeology, but will certainly consider books about the Aleutians.

The economics of publishing are such that it is getting harder and harder to publish site monographs and basic reports on field research, without hefty subsidies. More and more of such publication is migrating to the Web (see Chapter 12), which raises complex issues of accessibility in the long-term future. Fortunately, there are still some superb exceptions, among them Andrew Moore et al.'s *Village by the Euphrates: From Foraging to Farming at Abu Hureyra* (New York: Oxford University Press, 2000), a monograph on one of the earliest farming villages in the world in Syria, and *Hell Gap: A Stratified Paleoindian Campsite at the Edge of the Rockies*, edited by Mary Lou Larson, Marcel

Kornfeld, and George Frison (Salt Lake City: University of Utah Press, 2009), which summarizes years of Paleoindian work.

Increasingly, monographic publications are coming out under specialized imprints—notably British Archaeological Reports (BAR)—which are both national and international. Some presses on the Continent are still publishing site reports, to their eternal credit, as are some museums and university departments. In the long-term, however, site reports are going to migrate to the Web (see Chapter 12).

Synthetic works aimed at scholarly audiences are alive and well and will continue to appear as long as libraries will buy them. Very few of these books achieve sales of more than 1,000 to 3,000 copies over many years, but they are vital to professionals and students as state-of-the-art summaries of different areas. The same rules for submitting proposals and specimen chapters apply here as for more general works, with the exception that peer reviews will be part of the process. Again, this can be very helpful, especially when a proposal is involved and you are still actively shaping your book. As with trade books, you need to pay careful attention to competing volumes in the marketplace. You'll find potential competitors displayed at professional meetings, and you should be prepared to present a specific assessment of each and every one in your proposal. Remember that publishers expect to make money off your book, albeit a modest sum. This means that they have to ensure that the content is new, unique, and marketable.

Edited Volumes

As is apparent from these pages, I dislike edited volumes, which are usually compiled as a result of a session at a professional meeting or as a festschrift for some retiring scholar. If you write for an edited volume, be aware that such contributions might carry less weight with tenure review committees than an article in a peer-reviewed journal. The rules for writing these are the same as for academic journal articles, but with one exception, best posed as a question. How does your individual chapter relate to the overall theme of the book and to the other papers therein? This is, obviously, the editor's job, but it is also yours. All too often, edited volumes are mishmashes of miscellaneous contributions, many of which either bear no relevance to the subject matter of the volume or would best be published in a specialized journal. To avoid this pitfall, ask the volume editor for a complete outline of the book and specifically what role your chapter is expected to play in it. Also, make sure the editor has a commitment from a publisher before investing your time in writing a chapter for the volume. Only write for an edited volume if you really care about the subject matter and have complete confidence in the editor.

In the final analysis, academic writing is just the same as that for more general audiences. Clear exposition, a vigorous writing style, and a well-told, albeit technical story are essential ingredients of all archaeological writing. Again, let's once again remember Strunk and White: "Vigorous writing is concise. A statement should contain no unnecessary words, a paragraph no unnecessary sentences" (Strunk and White 2008 [1972]:ix). This is particularly true of writing in the digital world, which we discuss in Chapter 12.

AND NOW WE GO DIGITAL . . .

Rule 12: Think in screens but write nicely.

'VE JUST FINISHED WRITING *Elixir: A Human History of Water*, a book that has occupied my every waking moment for the past two years. *Elixir's* a linear narrative that begins with hunter-gatherers and ends with the Industrial Revolution. A story, yes, straightforward, no, for I had to confront issues of continuity and the need to cover widely separated areas within a single narrative framework. In the end, the story worked out well, but not without some fancy literary footwork along the way. There were moments when I wondered—and I still wonder—what would have happened if I'd written the book for the Web. With all the options available through digital media, it would have been very different.

Just a few sentences from the preface reveal tantalizing possibilities:

> As I researched *Elixir*, I was struck by how little most people's relationships with water changed over the thousands of years from the first appearance of agriculture some 12,000 years ago into medieval times and beyond. Even today, millions of subsistence farmers live from harvest to harvest, from one rainy season to the next, dependent on unpredictable water supplies from the heavens. (Fagan in press: xi)

Imagine these few words uncoupled from the linear narrative. The statement that people's relationships with water changed little for thousands of years arouses your curiosity. How can he be right? In the digital preface, there would be a hyperlink taking you to an animated chronological table, which sets out key developments, complete with links that take you to more detailed information about them. The sentence with "subsistence farmers live from harvest to harvest" would hyperlink you to material that covers the realities of subsistence farmers, with examples, including extracts from medieval documents and classic anthropological studies of subsistence farmers. Right from the beginning of the digital book, you are free to probe deeper, choose your own path through the history of water, and even go directly to details of Inca water management if you wish. The possibilities are truly intoxicating, even if they still lie somewhat in the future. I think we're on the threshold of a golden age of publishing and writing, but it's going to be very different from the familiar environment of today.

The dream is captivating and captures the imagination—a writing universe freed from the tyranny of the linear narrative. Actually, it's no dream, for it already exists in the now readily accessible digital world, which is yours for the exploration. But the vision is still very fresh and exploratory. Even when the first edition of this book appeared a mere five years ago, things digital were still a novelty. Web sites were already commonplace, but blogs, Twitter, and Facebook were barely figments of anyone's imagination. The word "revolution" has been overused in archaeology, as anyone who has studied the "Neolithic Revolution" well knows. But the move to cyberspace promises a true revolution in archaeological writing. Let me confess at once that I have never written anything significant for the Web beyond material for my web page and occasional blogs. This chapter, unlike its predecessors, is not based on practical experience. However, it offers a sampling of the opportunities that lie before us, which are truly exciting.

Away from the Linear Narrative

Digital media are a natural for archaeologists, who have long wanted to move away from linear story lines. Our excavations and field surveys, even our laboratory research, provide the basis for multiple narratives, multiple connections—what Ian Hodder of post-processual fame calls diverse "voices." Think of archaeological data at different scales: the environmental setting and the surrounding landscape, the site or sites themselves, major occupation levels, minor lenses representing a brief visit, individual features, artifact associations and food remains. The mosaic of evidence, of analysis and interpretation, is open-ended and never complete.

Any archaeological site is a palimpsest of collective and individual human experience preserved in material form. Writing a linear narrative, even with evocative descriptions and lyrical prose, provides but one perspective. Digital media give you a matrix way of communicating, where different means of presentation can link archaeological finds in ways that were hitherto virtually impossible. Recently, Syrian music scholar Ziad Ajjan composed eight poems and three musical fragments from a cuneiform tablet of 1400 B.C. found at the coastal city of Ugarit. The "Hymn of Supplication" tablet contains not only the music and words, but also performance instructions for the singer and a harpist. There are even instructions for tuning the harp. This splendid research has open-ended possibilities for digital exploration and presentation. Think of the links one could create to explore the art and music of 3,500 years ago, also literature, writing, and ancient thinking about archives—all this without stretching the evidence. Using an electronic forum, you can explore new theoretical approaches, argue about the classification of an artifact with three-dimensional, revolving images in front of everyone, or give colleagues a tour of your three-week excavation as it unfolds. All of this can form part of the permanent record of a research project. And, above all, you can use it to communicate to far larger, more diverse audiences than you will ever reach in print.

With digital media, you take your readers away from the extended narrative, the advertising-laden pages of a magazine, the imposed order of numbered pages in a book. Instead, you work with a matrix, which starts at an arbitrarily chosen point, which allows you, the writer or readers, to follow your or their individual interests, using hyperlinks. All of this is very different from writing an article or a book, for there is a great deal more to it than merely uploading your text to the

Web. You're entering a world of interaction, of constant dialogue with others, often complete strangers.

This new and completely unfamiliar writing world is going to change the way we think about writing an archaeological story. There will always be a framework, probably in the form of a hyperlinked narrative, but it will be short, designed to provide an overall plan to a complex and open-ended matrix. We now know enough about digital communication to realize that presenting information this way is very different from the familiar pathways of the printed word. All of us now live in a world of brevity and shortened attention spans, which provide the context for digital communication.

Earlier in this book, I wrote about the solitary world of the writer, closeted as one is in a quiet study, accompanied by books, piles of paper, probably a cat, and, as an esteemed colleague reminds me, sometimes some bourbon. Yes, you will sometimes still write alone, but instead of long narratives you'll be working almost entirely in individual screens (pages, if you will), at the most two or three at a time. Also, you'll now be writing a great deal of interactive material, which will involve continual collaboration with such folks as game designers, photographers, IT specialists, videographers, and web designers, as well as yourself, "the writer." Authorship has a whole new definition in this brave new world. Your most vital task will be to create a team of people who can produce multimedia materials that meld seamlessly with your narratives. If I go that route, and I'm sure I'll have to one day, my cat will have to share my study with a lot more people.

Once your article or book appears, such solitude as you still have won't last long. You'll be exposed to a cacophony of diverse readers. Forget the occasional e-mail from colleagues or readers offering comment or—more often, alas—pointing out errors. The very nature of digital media means that your work, if properly presented, will foster comment and debate, contributions from others—fellow specialists, scientists in other disciplines interested in your work, students, and the general public. Many of these comments will be trite, often useless, but among them will be gems from people with no connections with archaeology at all. Of course, much of your work will not provoke comment, but you are no longer the solitary writer in a cloistered room. You're part of a huge, amorphous cyber community. Much of the endless talk about the public communication of archaeology is outdated when effectively anyone with an interest in that past in general and in your work in particular can access it with a few keywords and computer strokes.

Digital writing is collaborative writing, the art of engaging with others and keeping conversations going. Another point: your texts are never fixed, always requiring updating. They are never locked as they are in a printed article or book. The content changes, needs updating, as a result both of new research and of interactions with your readers. You acquire a lifelong commitment to writing and posting constant updates to your original work and to your web sites. Out-of-date, unattended web sites are rarely consulted.

Writing in the Digital World

For all its startling possibilities, the same general rules for aspiring writers apply, with some differences. Content is what visitors to your work are looking for, which means that it should never be an afterthought, or merely captions to vivid illustrations. Instead of using a few words to link paragraphs or different sections of a chapter, you have to think from the beginning in terms of individual screens. These screens may form a sequence, or simply be the jumping-off point for the reader to follow his or her interests, but they must offer significant content, be clearly written, and be devoid of the usual sins—jargon, long sentences, and passive tenses.

When developing lectures or multimedia presentations—and I do have firsthand experience of this—detailed outlines are of paramount importance. The same applies even more forcefully here. Instead of outlines, perhaps you should think of the storyboards used by movie producers, which integrate both graphics and words to highlight individual scenes. An outline composed of a sequence of page synopses, comprising specs for audio, pictures, hyperlinks, simulations, video, and so on, works very effectively. As a general rule, the more precise your outline, the easier it will be to compose your final screens. The outline will also serve as a blueprint for the index to your digital presentation, however long it is. Think Table of Contents, but much more comprehensive—something that is user-friendly, hierarchical, and branching, and as open-ended as the publication.

This new medium still demands that you write with your usual passion and revise as carefully as you would for hard copy. After all, it's just as important to engage the reader in cyberspace as it is in print.

SOME SECRETS OF DIGITAL WRITING

- Write clearly and vividly, also with passion, just as you do in conventional writing.

- Think interaction with your readers and opportunities for interactivity and dialogue.

- Communicate information in much shorter chunks, writing in screens, or paragraph-sized amounts.

- Break things into sound bites, not long paragraphs or chapters.

- Provide numerous options for following different narratives based on readers' interests.

- Use diverse sources from the Web to round out pieces of the story.

- Make as much use of audio and visual materials as possible (but each image presented should provide useful information).

- Provide technical definitions and more specialized material by hyperlink.

- Revise! Revise! Revise!

Most of This Lies in the Future

So far, I've assumed that digital publishing is commonplace in archaeology, but it still isn't. Of course we all use e-mail, consult the Web, and even take online courses, but true digital publishing is quite a different beast. I'm dying to explore the realm of digital writing, which extends far beyond web sites into true interactivity, but it is likely to be a few more years before such efforts join the mainstream, especially of academic publishing. Here conservative mind-sets prevail, with promotion committees clinging longingly to the notion that the only legitimate publishing format is that of a printed, peer-reviewed book, preferably released by a university press, the more prestigious the better. This is nonsense, of course, in a world where more and more journals, including the *Proceedings of the National Academy of Science*, publish peer-reviewed articles online. One only hopes that younger generations of scholars will embrace new perspectives on what constitutes "legitimate," peer-reviewed publication. In this day and age, a bold, experimental digital book-length publication of an important piece of cutting-edge research, duly peer-reviewed, is just as likely to have a significant impact as a conventional book. If nothing else, a lot of people who would otherwise never look at such things will probably read parts of it. However, until academic attitudes change, the action in much digital book publication will remain at the periphery, where it is already beginning to flourish.

In one sense, I cannot blame promotion committees for being cautious, for the advent of the Web has led to a quantum jump in books placed online, including a lot of very poor archaeology and what can, at best, be charitably described as pseudo-archaeology and arrant nonsense. The solution is rigorous peer-review, which provides a reasonably effective check-and-balance of academic quality. But if ever there was a place where *caveat emptor* (Latin: "buyer beware") applies, it is the digital world.

We're moving inexorably into digital publishing. Confronted with rising costs and shrinking library budgets, most serious academic publishers, including the most prestigious in the land, are becoming ever more selective in their acceptances for hard-copy books. From the archaeological perspective, this is a particularly acute problem for such books as site monographs, which are punishingly expensive to produce and never sell in large numbers. Publication subsidies are ever rarer, too. Yet the analyses and raw data in such reports are of vital importance for future generations of fieldworkers. Then there's the enduring problem of the so-called grey literature, much of it CRM reports of limited accessibility despite a network of repositories. Large parts of the answer to these problems reside in the digital realm, provided that quality issues can be resolved.

Digital books bristle with formidable problems like storage, which is why the Mellon Foundation has funded the Archaeology of the Americas Digital Monograph Initiative run by a half-dozen university presses. The Initiative aims to develop and publish a new generation of peer-reviewed monographs that will incorporate—in a stable on-line environment—what the participants call "enhanced data sets" that support scholarly analyses and interpretation. These may include data collection sheets, databases, digital still- and moving-image files (such as color GIS maps, 3D laser scans, rotatable objects, and video clips) and supplementary text. To quote their web page: "AADMI will ini-tially focus on book-length works authored or edited by junior schol-ars in the field of New World archaeology. AADMI publications shall be available on a digital delivery platform that permits, within reason-able limits, the search, display, updating, analysis, and downloading of digital monographs and their associated data sets" (http://www. archaeologyoftheamericas.com). AADMI will facilitate partnerships with other digital initiatives to optimize the effectiveness and impact of its projects. Finally, AADMI envisions the production of enhanced monographs as a true instance of multi-platform design and delivery, with print and digital editions appearing concurrently. Wisely, the initial focus is on junior scholars, for these are the ones who will be leaders in the digital world of archaeology. The project is still in its setup phase. As of the time of writing, no monographs have yet been published.

All of this adds up to a fascinating new world of writing and pub-lication, which may well lead to a golden age. But I'm likely to be pushing up daisies before it achieves any semblance of maturity—if ever it does, so continual and dizzying are the changes. I only hope I have a chance to write something significant for cyberspace before I depart. Anyone embarking on serious writing today is crazy if they don't think digital.

Some Digital Formats

Social networking is all the fashion these days. Facebook, LinkedIn, Twitter, and such platforms grab the headlines. *Archaeology Magazine*, even Left Coast Press, maintain social networking sites. Such formats have limited use for snippets of archaeological news and are also a means of developing a readership. Facebook and its equivalents can become utterly time-consuming, indeed obsessive. Personally, I steer clear, partly because I value my privacy and also because I spend far too much time at the computer as it is. But social networking has the advantage of immediacy and provides extended networking. You can pose questions to, and get answers from, a global community, often in minutes. This immediacy, this ability to broadcast to, and receive feedback from, folks around the world was impossible until now.

Blogs, aimed at either fellow archaeologists or the general public, have become a fashionable way of commenting on discoveries, field seasons, and so on. They are a good way of reaching the wider audience about what archaeologists really do and of counteracting the nonsense that so often passes for archaeology in cyberspace.

Blogs of field projects are all the rage, providing as they do an immediacy unknown even a generation ago. Your findings and interpretations can be broadcast worldwide while you are still in the trenches. But there's always a danger that your initial assessment will prove wrong on more sober reflection. A classic case revolved around the recent discovery of a large woman's tomb in Britain. Someone remarked that maybe she was a female gladiator. Instant headlines hit international newsstands. The excavator soon admitted that he had no proof that the woman was anything more than an oversized female. The resulting press coverage was minimal.

There's another side to the excavation blog, where immediacy can be of great benefit. Your blogs make the excavation process highly visible. Outsiders can see what you're doing, where your data comes from and how good it is, and how you arrive at your interpretations. This is a far cry from a casual remark to a journalist that hits the headlines. You're sharing thought processes, not necessarily conclusions, which is a healthy intellectual process.

Writing a blog is straightforward. Keep it short, use the first person, and express your opinions about your topic at hand. Make it provocative if you can, so that you generate commentary and responses. (To be frank, though, most comments on my blog contribute little or nothing to serious dialogue.) Illustrations are an excellent idea, especially if you are talking about sites you have visited.

Blogs work best if you think of them as a form of conversation. In part they are a form of "social networking," but they are far more for many people. Digital journalists anxious to create a significant readership spend many hours developing contacts and networking with all manner of people. This is known as "creating a platform," a readership. A platform is all-important for a journalist and a significant issue for anyone who wants to communicate archaeology to as wide an audience as possible. As K. Kris Hirst of archaeology.about.com—who knows far more about this than I—remarked to me, it's defining your area of expertise, giving yourself what she calls a "marketable identity," that helps you connect to people interested in similar things. A classic example is the author Julie Powell, who developed a blog describing her attempts to cook all the recipes in Julia Child's *Mastering the Art of French Cooking* (rev. ed., New York: Alfred Knopf, 2001). She aimed her blog at baby boomers who remembered Child fondly, at people who like to cook but not professionally, and writer wannabes. Her resulting book, *Julie and Julia: A Year of Cooking Dangerously* (Boston: Little, Brown, 2009), became a best seller.

You can't sustain an effective blog by relying only on people who know you personally or have read your work. How, then, do you ensure that others find you, that search engines recognize you and your content? You need to learn about search engines and how they work. Web crawlers look for keywords, not such generic topics as "archaeology," but much finer grades of keywords. This means that you have to design your web page and your blogs, as well as your writing style, to help search engines recognize your content. Choosing keywords is a fine art and requires careful thought. For instance, if you use "elixir" as a keyword, you are probably but one of hundreds, if not thousands, of people using the same word to identify their sites. "Elixir History of Water" will really narrow the search. Another consideration is the audience you want to reach. If you use a technical keyword like "Roman calix" (or calyx), you'll identify your site as academic, and only scholars will find you. So pay careful attention to keywords, far more than you would with a conventional article. Tags are also important.

You should make it easy for people to tag your blog pages or web sites for visibility at Delicious, Facebook, and elsewhere. Links to other web sites are important. Create as many such links as you can to attract people to your site.

Web sites come in every shape and size, and cover every kind of archaeological topic imaginable, from excavations and such esoterica as lithic analysis to tourism and heritage. The problem is in finding them. No one can possibly keep track of all the archaeological web sites out there. If you develop a web site, pay careful attention to keywords, tags, as so on, just as you do for a blog.

SOME KEY ARCHAEOLOGICAL WEB SITES

- ArchNet, run by Arizona State University, at http://archnet.asu. edu/, is an international virtual library of archaeology, which everyone should bookmark.

- The European equivalent is ARGE (The Archaeological Resource Guide for Europe), at http://odur.let.rug.nl/arge/.

- *Archaeology Magazine* maintains an excellent list of major archaeological web sites, including some recommendations from their staff, at www.archaeology.org/wwwarky/index.html.

- Another useful source is Archaeology Online, at http://www. archaeologyonline.net.

- The Center for the Study of Architecture offers interesting perspectives at http://csanet.org.

- The Digital Archaeological Record addresses the issue of raw data, at http://www.tdar.org/confluence/display.TDAR/Home. It is a digital repository designed to both preserve and enhance access to digital records of archaeological investigations.

(Of course there are many more. . . .)

There is far more to a web site than merely putting up some pictures and a brief narrative. There are some excellent narrative-only sites, such as Explorator, which provides a weekly summary of archaeological discoveries and news, including obituaries. You can access it at http://tech.groups.yahoo.com/group/Explorator/, or subscribe at Explorator-subscribe@yahoogroups.com. This is well worth subscribing to (for free), just to keep you up-to-date. Some of the best sites provide ongoing updates of excavations and other happenings. I've always enjoyed the Çatalhöyük web site covering this important excavation in Turkey, where you can access archived reports, tour the excavations, and learn the latest news: http://www.catalhoyuk.com/. This is a classic example of a dynamic research project that involves far more than just the research team, encourages alternative narratives, and draws the local community and the public into the project.

Designing a web page requires skills that I don't have, so I rely on a professional graphic designer for mine (brianfagan.com). It's well worth the expense. Professionals know what attracts visitors and how to make the site visually appealing. They can also navigate the realm of keywords and tags. Many archaeological web sites are drab and clearly amateurish productions, when the expenditure of even a modest sum would make them so much better. A good webmaster will also know how to optimize your site so that it's picked up by search engines. He or she will also advise you on keywords.

Be sure to keep your web site up-to-date. Otherwise it leaves a deafening message that you're not that interested.

The best way to learn about web sites is to use them. Open Google, choose some keywords, and go. The esoteric information available online is truly fascinating. Only the other day, I learned all about "futtock shrouds."

E-Books, Not Just Kindles

Anyone who travels extensively or goes into the field should acquire a Kindle, iPad, or other form of electronic reader. These devices allow you to carry huge numbers of book with you at low cost, all with the weight of a single paperback. Kindles and their equivalents are transforming the publishing business, but at present they are little more than electronic versions of printed books. They are easy to read, but have disadvantages, notably often poor picture quality. But I'm addicted and am reading much more serious nonfiction than I used to. Electronic book readers are here to stay, and I'll always own one for its convenience.

But there's potentially far more to e-books than you can get from a Kindle. E-books have huge potential advantages for archaeologists. Visually alone, the prospects make one drool—the ability to use color, to include as many visuals as you wish, to incorporate video. You can use interactive maps, reproduce them at very large scales, and develop animated drawings and three-dimensional graphics that allow you to examine artifacts from any angle. Digital books will contain far more information than any printed one, including access to enormous databases of both processed and raw information. The format allows the reader to navigate through a site report or a survey monograph in multiple ways, allowing one to focus on, say, backed blades or certain pottery types.

Mitch Allen pointed out another potential advantage of e-books: the ability to take your entire reference library to the field, in order to do more comparative analysis on-site rather than bringing back materials to the lab—provided you have electricity. As the roles of authorship change over the next decade, there will be people who create corpuses of material for this purpose, such as complete sets of all published Maya stelae or Greek rhytons (vessels for pouring libations) in a single database for anyone who needs it in the field.

Digital books sound like an archaeologist's dream, but they come with some serious potential problems. You can, of course, just put something up on the Web and never revisit it, but that's a cop-out and a denial of the vibrant nature of cyberspace. If your book is a permanent presence there, it's important not because it's there, but because of its content. Realize that your digital book is a living entity, which will haunt you for the rest of your life. Readers will use the data, interact with the content, and ask you questions. You'll need to be constantly alert for bugs, which need to be fixed quickly. You'll be endlessly updating both text and visuals, inserting new interpretations and fresh perspectives resulting from later discoveries. You'll need to develop some system of making sure that there is only one edition of the book on the Web—the latest one. And then you'll still have to devise a way for the reader to know which version he or she is using. Fortunately, there are other fields that are already deeply involved with digital books, so many of the more serious bugs and problems with revision will be worked out before we archaeologists become major players.

If you're prepared to commit yourself to an e-book, you'll be the proud author of a living, vibrant work that is always fresh in its perspectives and should never fall out of date. Think what archaeology would be like if digital publication had been around for a half-century or more. Take, for example, the case of the Cambridge University archaeologist Grahame Clark's *Star Carr* (Cambridge University Press, 1954), a classic monograph on this most famous of European Mesolithic sites. Imagine if Clark had been able to create a digital book in 1954. By now, a whole range of talented archaeologists would have added to the original monograph with new data, fresh interpretations—with the expectation that future generations of archaeologists would also add their work.

In the long-term future, I think that a significant number of digital monographs will be permanent, ever-changing phenomena, which become the work not of one author, but of generations of researchers, with overall responsibility for maintaining the integrity of the book lying in the hands of a single individual. Such a model is but a dream at this stage, but it's already feasible technologically. Yet it will require major changes in our mind-sets as authors, where monographs, even more than they are today, become long-term partnerships among archaeologists, some of whom may already be dead, and, eventually, others not yet born—a slightly alarming thought. You always have a stake in any book you have written, but unless a hard-copy work goes to multiple editions, you never get to revisit it. With a digital book, you are on board forever. If you're not, it will show up like a sore thumb when researchers consult your work.

In the end, it all comes down to the issue of permanence. The digital book sounds wonderful in theory, but just how permanent is it? What can you do to ensure true permanence in the face of outdated software that becomes unreadable or computer records that have deteriorated in storage? I once went to a historians' conference at Stanford

University where much of the conversation concerned deteriorated and now inaccessible computer records from the 1960s. This question is still unresolved, but should not deter us from exploring the digital realm, for, in the end, permanence will be achieved. It has to be. One possible solution lies in the increasing prevalence of cloud computing, whereby the risk is spread over a constellation of servers and software alternatives. (Cloud computing is a distributed hardware infrastructure and software equivalents.) For instance, if you use gmail, your messages are held by cloud computing networks. This may help resolve long-term problems of data impermanence and migration to new formats.

Now we can upload data when we wish, publish inexpensively, and put forth our stories of the past or pet theories whenever we wish—virtually without cost. But this new-fangled ease of communication makes high academic standards and really good writing even more important than before. And the latter is what this book's about.

CONCLUSION

AFTER SIX DRAFTS, massive (and invaluable) editorial input, and significant moments of literary despair, I've finally reached the end of the second edition of *Writing Archaeology*. Once again, I've learned the hard way that no one learns to write all at once. On the contrary, I seem to reinvent my writing every time I sit at a computer or have a new experience. I've learned that the skill of writing is no gift from God, but something acquired by years of practice—and even then you keep on learning. What really matters is how you say things, and how thoroughly you rewrite your prose to say something clearly and in a good, economical way. Reading this book won't solve all your writing problems; no one but you can do this. Improvement won't come unless you work at your writing, open yourself to criticism, and act upon it, so—write, write!

We archaeologists have lost sight of distant horizons, of the great issues of our discipline. We need to write for humanity, for civilization, not just for our friends—and our enemies. And that's why I had the temerity to write this book.

RESOURCES FOR WRITERS

The resources that follow are but a sample of what's available and are intended as an introduction to a huge body of information.

General Writing

The literature is ever-proliferating and it's difficult to know where to begin, but I suggest starting with:

- Zinsser, William. 1990. *On Writing Well.* New York: Harper Perennial.
  Eminently down-to-earth and enjoyable.

The following three volumes are key reference works, updated annually, that may be of use. Most public libraries have them, so you can always consult the latest editions:

- Brewer, Robert Lee. 2009. *2010 Writer's Market.* New York: Writer's Digest Books.
  A comprehensive and reliable resource. Or you can select *2010 Writer's Market Deluxe* by the same publisher, which includes access to Web-based materials and a magazine subscription.

- Sambuchino, Chuck. 2009. *2010 Guide to Literary Agents.* New York: Writer's Digest Books.
  Self-evident. Includes online access to listings.

■ Turner, Barry. 2010. *The Writer's Handbook, 2011*. London and New York: Palgrave Macmillan.

> UK-based but very useful. As the London *Times* puts it: "wise and witty."

Style and Technicalities

■ *The Chicago Manual of Style*. 2010. 16th ed. Chicago: University of Chicago Press.

> This definitive and monumental work is the bible for the rules of English usage. The *Chicago Manual* has been around since 1906 and is used by most publishing houses. Invest in a copy whatever writing you do.

Dictionaries are legion, starting with the *Oxford English Dictionary*, which is, however, a British English dictionary. There are numerous American choices. In my view, the best are:

■ *The American Heritage Dictionary of the English Language*. 2006. 4th ed. Boston: Houghton Mifflin.

■ *The New Oxford American Dictionary*. 2005. 2nd ed. New York: Oxford University Press.

■ There are many dictionary sources on the Web, such as Dictionary. com.

■ A copy of *Roget's 21st Century Thesaurus* (New York: Dell, 2005) is useful, but most word-processing programs have very adequate thesaurus features.

Indexing

The web site www.anindexer.com has useful basic information on indexing and software.

Writing Proposals

■ Rabiner, Susan, and Alfred Fortunato. 2002. *Thinking Like Your Editor: How to Write Great Serious Non-Fiction—and Get It Published.* New York: W.W. Norton.

This is the single best source on ideas and proposal writing, whatever your subject matter. If you're serious about writing, buy this book at once and make it your bible.

Academic Writing

These titles may be of use for general archaeological writing, but they are aimed primarily at authors of academic books.

■ Becker, Howard S. 2007. *Writing for Social Scientists: How to Start and Finish Your Thesis, Book, or Article.* 2nd ed. Chicago: University of Chicago Press.

A favorite that is aimed at academic writers and students.

■ Derricourt, Robin. 1996. *An Author's Guide to Scholarly Publishing.* Princeton, NJ: Princeton University Press.

Derricourt is both an archaeologist and a publisher, which makes this book doubly useful. It's crammed full of useful advice and written in an entertaining way. Also recommended for the "Writing about Archaeology" section.

■ Luey, Beth. 2009. *Handbook for Academic Authors.* 5th ed. Cambridge: Cambridge University Press.

A fundamental source for all specialist authors and students, it contains much of value for the more general writer.

■ Matthews, J. R., J. M. Bowen, and R. W. Matthews. 2001. *Successful Scientific Writing: A Step-by-Step Guide for the Biological and Medical Sciences.* 2nd ed. Cambridge: Cambridge University Press.

This is exactly what the title says it is. Helpful for the more technical writer.

Textbook Writing

These three books cover the material in Chapter 9 in more detail, with an emphasis on the nitty-gritty.

- Lepionka, Mary Ellen. 2008. *Writing and Developing Your College Textbook*. 2nd ed. Gloucester, MA: Atlantic Path Publishing.

- Lepionka, Mary Ellen. 2005. *Writing and Developing College Textbook Supplements*. Gloucester, MA: Atlantic Path Publishing.

- Silverman, Franklin H. 2004. *Self-Publishing Textbooks and Instructional Materials*. Gloucester, MA: Atlantic Path Publishing.

Writing about Archaeology

There is almost no directly relevant literature, but these are of use:

- Allen, Mitch. 2002. Reaching the Hidden Audience: Ten Rules for the Archaeological Writer. In *The Public Benefits of Archaeology*, ed. Barbara J. Little, pp. 244–251. Gainesville: University of Florida Press.

- Allen, Mitchell, and Rosemary Joyce. 2010. Communicating Archaeology in the 21st Century. In *Voices in American Archaeology*, ed. Wendy Ashmore, Dorothy Lippert, and Barbara J. Mills, pp. 270–290. Washington, DC: SAA Press.

- Berger, Stefan, H. Feldner, and K. Passmore. 2003. *Writing History: Theory and Practice*. London: Edward Arnold.

  A useful volume that surveys historical writing, discussing problems also encountered by archaeologists.

- Connah, Graham. 2010. *Writing about Archaeology*. Cambridge: Cambridge University Press.

  Connah distills a lifetime's experience of writing about the past into an admirable introduction for all kinds of archaeology writers. This book is especially good on academic writing.

■ Joyce, Rosemary, et al. 2002. *The Languages of Archaeology: Dialogue, Narrative, and Writing*. Oxford: Blackwell.

The authors examine theoretical issues faced when writing about archaeology. Not of great use for general archaeological writers.

■ Zimmerman, Larry J. 2003. *Presenting the Past*. Walnut Creek, CA: AltaMira Press.

This common-sense paperback is volume 7 of The Archaeologist's Toolkit series and discusses some of the issues covered in this book.

Archaeological Illustration

There are a considerable number of specialist guides, but the following have wide application:

■ Adkins, Lesley, and Roy A. Adkins. 1989. *Archaeological Illustration*. Cambridge: Cambridge University Press.

A useful general survey.

■ Dillon, Brian, ed. 1985. *The Student's Guide to Archaeological Illustrating*. Los Angeles: UCLA Institute of Archaeology.

Excellent, if you can find it.

■ Dorrell, Peter G. 1995. *Photography in Archaeology and Conservation*. 2nd ed. Cambridge: Cambridge University Press.

A standard work.

■ Hart, Russell, and Dan Richards. 2003. *Photography for Dummies*. 2nd ed. New York: Wiley.

■ King, Julie Adair, and Serge Timachoff. 2008. *Digital Photography for Dummies*. 6th ed. New York: John Wiley.

Archaeological Reference Books

You'll be surprised how often you need to check a fact, a site, a person. A blizzard of archaeological encyclopedias and similar reference works have descended on us in recent years, but I would recommend:

■ Bahn, Paul, ed. 2001. *The Penguin Archaeology Guide*. London: Penguin Books.

> This is especially good for sites and cultures. Despite its title, this is more of an archaeological dictionary than a guide.

■ Bintcliff, John, ed. 2004. *A Companion to Archaeology*. Oxford: Blackwell.

> Bintcliff has assembled a galaxy of sound archaeologists to write sensibly about a broad array of topics from genetics to green issues. Longer essays make for a good survey of major controversies.

■ Cunliffe, Barry, Chris Gosden, and Rosemary Joyce, eds. 2009. *The Oxford Handbook of Archaeology*. Oxford: Oxford University Press.

> Another reference book that covers all aspects of archaeology in authoritative essays.

■ Fagan, Brian, ed. 1996. *The Oxford Companion to Archaeology*. New York: Oxford University Press.

> A compendium of articles long and short about every kind of archaeological topic imaginable by leading experts. A little outdated, but still authoritative.

■ Scarre, Chris, ed. 1988. *Past Worlds: The Times Atlas of Archaeology*. London: Times Books.

> The best archaeological atlas in the world.

Writing Magazines

These tend to cater to the hopeful, but sometimes contain interesting ideas and tips.

■ *Writer's Digest* (www.writersdigest.com)

■ *Writer's Magazine* (www.writersservices.com)

■ *Burning Void* (www.burningvoid.com/links/4) has links to writer's magazines.

Web Resources

We discussed some basic archaeological web sites in Chapter 11. As far as writing for the Web is concerned, here are some resources. The options are legion, their reliability often dubious, but the following will be invaluable.

There are dozens of books about writing for the Web; these seem to be the best at the moment:

■ Alexander, Janet E., and Marsha Ann Tate. 2009. *Web Wisdom: How to Evaluate and Create Information Quality on the Web*. 2nd ed. Boca Raton, FL: CRC Press.

■ Redish, Janice. 2007. *Letting Go of the Words: Writing Web Content that Works* (Interactive Technologies). Menlo Park, CA: Morgan Kaufmann.

Creative-writing instructors and organizations compile many useful web sites. Here are two sources out of many:

■ Online Resources for Writers (http://webster.commnet.edu/writing/writing.htm)

A list of useful items compiled by an English professor.

- Internet Resources-Writers Resources (www.internet-resources.com/
  writers)

  This lists the "100 best" resources for writers and will take you
  almost anywhere you want to go.

REFERENCES

Adovasio, J., and J. Page. 2002. *The First Americans: In Pursuit of Archaeology's Greatest Mystery.* New York: Random House.

Balter, M. 2004. *The Goddess and the Bull: Çatalhöyük: An Archaeological Journey to the Dawn of Civilization.* New York: Free Press.

Brumm, A. 2010. "The Falling Sky": Symbolic and Cosmological Associations of the Mt. William Greenstone Axe Quarry, Central Victoria, Australia. *Cambridge Archaeological Journal* 20(2): 179–196.

Carter, H., and A. C. Mace. 1923. *The Tomb of Tut.ankh.amen Discovered by the Late Earl of Carnarvon and Howard Carter,* Vol. 1. London: Macmillan.

Clark, J. G. D. 1954. *Excavations at Star Carr: An Early Mesolithic Site at Seamer near Scarborough, Yorkshire.* Cambridge: Cambridge University Press.

——. 1961. *World Prehistory.* Cambridge: Cambridge University Press.

Cline, E. H. 2000. *The Battles of Armageddon: Megiddo and the Jezreel Valley from the Bronze Age to the Nuclear Age.* Ann Arbor: University of Michigan Press.

——. 2004. *Jerusalem Besieged: From Ancient Canaan to Modern Israel.* Ann Arbor: University of Michigan Press.

Diamond, J. 1997. *Guns, Germs, and Steel: The Fates of Human Societies.* New York: W.W. Norton.

Eiseley, L. 1971. *The Night Country.* New York: Charles Scribners.

Fagan, B. M. 1961. A Collection of Nineteenth Century Soli Ironwork from the Lusaka Area of Northern Rhodesia. *Journal of the Royal Anthropological Institute* 91(2):228–249.

——. 1969. *Iron Age Cultures in Zambia.* Vol. 2: *Dambwa, Ingombe Ilede, and the Tonga,* edited by B. M. Fagan, D. W. Phillipson, and S. G. H. Daniels. London: Chatto and Windus.

———. 1975. *The Rape of the Nile: Tomb Robbers, Tourists, and Archaeologists in Egypt*. New York: Charles Scribners.

———. 1977. *Clash of Cultures*. San Francisco: W.H. Freeman.

———. 1985. *The Adventure of Archaeology*. Washington, DC: National Geographic Society.

———. 1995. *Time Detectives: How Archaeologists Use Technology to Recapture the Past*. New York: Simon and Schuster.

———. 1998. *From Black Land to Fifth Sun: The Science of Sacred Sites*. Reading, MA: Helix.

———. 1999. *Floods, Famines, and Emperors: El Niño and the Fate of Civilizations*. New York: Basic Books.

———. 2000. *The Little Ice Age: How Climate Made History, 1300–1850*. New York: Basic Books.

———. 2003. *Before California: An Archaeologist Looks at our Earliest Inhabitants*. Walnut Creek, CA: AltaMira Press.

———. 2004a. *Ancient North America: The Archaeology of a Continent*. 4th ed. London: Thames & Hudson.

———. 2004b. *The Long Summer: How Climate Changed Civilization*. New York: Basic Books.

———. 2005. *Chaco Canyon: Archaeologists Explore the Lives of an Ancient Society*. New York: Oxford University Press.

———. 2006a. *Fish on Friday: Feasting, Fasting, and the Discovery of the New World*. New York: Basic Books.

———. 2009. *In the Beginning*. 12th ed. Upper Saddle River, NJ: Prentice Hall.

———. 2010a. *Ancient Lives: An Introduction to Archaeology and Prehistory*. 4th ed. Upper Saddle River, NJ: Prentice Hall.

———. 2010b. *Cro-Magnon: How the Ice Age Gave Birth to the First Modern Humans*. New York: Bloomsbury Press.

———. 2011. *Elixir: A Human History of Water*. New York: Bloomsbury Press.

Fagan, B. M., and K. Garrett. 2001. *Egypt of the Pharaohs*. Washington, DC: National Geographic Society.

Fox, J. A., and J. Levin. 1993. *How to Work with the Media*. Thousand Oaks, CA: Sage Publications.

Hodder, I. 2006. *The Leopard's Tale: Revealing the Mysteries of Çatalhöyük*. London: Thames and Hudson.

Huxley, T. H. 1863. *Man's Place in Nature*. New York: Appleton.

Johanson, D., and M. Edey. 1981. *Lucy: The Beginnings of Humankind*. New York: Simon and Schuster.

Kemp, B. 2006. *Ancient Egypt: The Anatomy of a Civilization*. Rev. ed. London: Routledge.

Kurlansky, M. 1997. *Cod: A Biography of the Fish That Changed the World*. New York: Walker.

Larson, M. L., M. Kornfeld, and G. Frison. 2009. *Hell Gap: A Stratified Paleoindian Campsite at the Edge of the Rockies*. Salt Lake City: University of Utah Press.

Layard, A. H. 1849. *Nineveh and Its Remains*. London: John Murray.

Lewis-Williams, D. 2002. *The Mind in the Cave: Consciousness and the Origins of Art*. London: Thames & Hudson.

McCarthy, C. 2005. *No Country for Old Men*. New York: Alfred Knopf.

Meltzer, D. 2009. *First Peoples in a New World: Colonizing Ice Age America*. Berkeley: University of California Press.

Moore, A., G. C. Hillman, and A. Legge. 2000. *Village by the Euphrates: From Foraging to Farming at Abu Hureyra*. New York: Oxford University Press.

Morison, S. E. 1942. *Admiral of the Ocean Sea*. Boston: Little, Brown.

Moseley, M. 2001. *The Incas and Their Ancestors: The Archaeology of Peru*. Rev. ed. London: Thames & Hudson.

Nöel Hume, I. 1982. *Martin's Hundred*. New York: Alfred Knopf.

Pryor, F. 2003. *Britain B.C.: Life in Britain and Ireland before the Romans*. London: HarperCollins.

Rabiner, S., and A. Fortunato. 2002. *Thinking Like Your Editor*. New York: W.W. Norton.

Roddick, A. P., and C. A. Hastorf. 2010. Tradition Brought to the Surface: Continuity, Innovation and Change in the Late Formative Period, Taraco Peninsula, Bolivia. *Cambridge Archaeological Journal* 20(2): 157–178.

Schele, L., and D. Freidel. 1990. *A Forest of Kings: The Untold Story of the Ancient Maya*. New York: William Morrow.

Strunk, W., and E. B. White. 2008 [1972]. *The Elements of Style*. 50th Anniversary Edition. New York: Longman, 2008.

Sobel, D. 1995. *Longitude: The True Story of a Lone Genius Who Solved the Greatest Scientific Problem of His Time*. New York: Walker.

Spector, J. 1993. *What This Awl Means: Feminist Archaeology at a Wahpeton Dakota Village*. Minneapolis: Minnesota Historical Society.

Stephens, J. L. 1843. *Incidents of Travel in Chiapas and Yucatan*. New York: Harpers.

Wheeler, M. 1943. *Maiden Castle*. London: Society of Antiquaries.

Wodehouse, P. G. 1919. *A Damsel in Distress*. London: Herbert Jenkins.

Wolcott, H. F. 2008. *Writing Up Qualitative Research*. 3rd ed. Thousand Oaks, CA: Sage Publications.

Woolley, L. 1929. *Ur of the Chaldees*. London: Ernest Benn.

Zimmerman, L. J. 2003. *Presenting the Past*. The Archaeologist's Toolkit 7. Walnut Creek, CA: AltaMira Press.

ABOUT THE AUTHOR

Brian Fagan is professor emeritus in the Department of Anthropology at the University of California, Santa Barbara. After studying archaeology at Pembroke College, Cambridge, he spent seven years doing archaeology and museum work in Central and East Africa, before coming to the United States in 1966. His original specialty was the African Iron Age, an esoteric subject if ever there was one, and he became involved in the founding of multidisciplinary African history. He came to the University of California, Santa Barbara, in 1967, and simultaneously changed intellectual directions, becoming a generalist who wrote about archaeology for general audiences. Since then, he has suffered through the writing of many books, including a series of widely used texts such as *In the Beginning* and *People of the Earth*. His numerous trade books include *The Rape of the Nile*, *The Adventure of Archaeology*, *The Little Ice Age*, *Fish on Friday*, and *Elixir: A Human History of Water*. His other interests include bicycling, cruising under sail, kayaking, good food, and cats. He and his family are (at last count) the proud owners of two cats, a horse, several mosquito fish, and seven rabbits.